Identify

Identify

Basic principles of identity design in the iconic trademarks of Chermayeff & Geismar

Published by Print Publishing

PRINT

Published by Print Publishing
an imprint of F+W Media, Inc.
38 East 29th Street, New York, NY
10016. (212) 447-1400.
First edition.

For more excellent design
information and resources, visit
www.printmag.com.

ISBN-13 (978-1-4403-1032-4)

15 14 13 12 11   5 4 3 2 1

Distributed in Canada
by Fraser Direct
100 Armstrong Avenue
Georgetown, Ontario
Canada L7G 5S4
Tel: (905) 877-4411

Distributed in the U.K. and Europe
by F&W Media International, LTD
Brunel House, Forde Close
Newton Abbot
TQ12 4PU, UK

Tel: (+44) 1626 323200
Fax: (+44) 1626 323319
Email: enquiries@fwmedia.com

Distributed in Australia
by Capricorn Link
P.O. Box 704, Windsor
NSW 2756
Australia
Tel: (02) 4577-3555

Edited by:
Aaron Kenedi

Designed by:
Chermayeff & Geismar

Contents

Preface

Some things in life come and go, but the Chermayeff & Geismar logos are eternal.

As a little boy, I was as much affected and reassured by the Chase Manhattan logo and the Mobil Oil sign as I was by the good parenting I received. And like parenting, the deeply felt presence of these iconic symbols was at times as disquieting as it was reassuring. Those iconic symbols were always in the background. They were omnipresent and dominant. Sometimes unnoticed, they were felt. In almost the exact same way as our parents, those monolithic, humorous, homogeneous logos raised us into the country we are, for good or bad.

The social implications of these logos are as varied as the products they represent. Airlines. TV studios. Oil companies. Banks. Arts associations. These are the shaping influences of our lives as Americans, and without those logos our world would have no physical identity. You can say they stand for the strongest part of our country, the pulling to the middle of all classes, all races, religions, and peoples. Large, simple shapes in standard clear-cut colors. Plain, honest images that would instill confidence in anyone. Order and strength. Leadership. Principles that reflect corporate culture, only after the fact of Chermayeff & Geismar. They taught Corporate America how to think.

It's the same thought as Life Imitating Art. First you have someone with a vision then you have history. Chermayeff & Geismar began designing clean iconic logos before the idea of what we refer to today as "branding." These symbols gave America something to live up to. Like a stunning psychic vision they knew the future and created it in advance. It is impossible to divorce emotions—even a touch of resentment—from these icons of Corporate America. Regardless of the social implications, they made the world a better-looking place with their presence. You could argue that they made us *modern*. The simplicity and wit of these symbols are the very definition of the word. They lived with us and represented us through America's most confident time and will live on into our uncertain future as symbols of our past glory.

Chermayeff & Geismar have given us a past and a future. All the things we get from our parents. And in the same way we look at our parents, the same way we love them, so we scrutinize and love these grand symbols of authority—with the gimlet eye of conditioned love.

Isaac Mizrahi

Foreword: Chermayeff & Geismar, the firm

Chermayeff & Geismar is one of America's most prolific graphic, interactive, and exhibition design firms. The two names on the marquee belong to the founders Ivan Chermayeff and Tom Geismar, who have defined American postwar modernism. When read together in one rhythmic cadence, the title also signifies an impressive selection and collection of individual designers who have comprised the firm and have impacted the history of communication design.

Chermayeff & Geismar has touched so many businesses and institutions with their signature brand of modernism and eclecticism—their precisionist designs and smart conceptions—that American business and culture would not be the same without the firm. It is impossible to walk down a midtown Manhattan sidewalk without seeing a wide array of their logos, posters, shopping bags, and other commercial and cultural artifacts, like the Chase Bank and Mobil Oil trademarks. Along with hundreds of other familiar graphic marks and identities, their contributions are indelible signposts—some are even iconic.

Yet to the public even the most routinely recognized graphic design is largely anonymous, with designers rarely acknowledged outside of a small professional circle. While many laymen and designers can quickly identify trademarks for the Public Broadcasting System, NBC, Showtime, and Barneys New York, or have seen the exhibition at the Ellis Island Immigration Museum, or will perhaps have snapshots taken next to the huge red nine in front of 9 West 57th Street, few people comprehend the authorship of these significant works.

Nonetheless it is necessary to acknowledge how Ivan Chermayeff, Tom Geismar, and their partners and associates have written—and along with partner Sagi Haviv continue to write—significant chapters in the graphic design legacy, from the 20th-century analog age through to the 21st-century digital age. Their collective influence on America's graphic design language cannot be overstated. This book is a record but also a testament. They have indeed made their mark with many marks. And they continue to do so.

Steven Heller

Introduction: a consistent approach in a changing world

Our first major trademark, the blue octagon we designed to identify Chase Manhattan Bank in 1960, was a simple bold form that could be carved into the sides of buildings, reproduced in small size on business cards, and printed in black-and-white newspaper ads around the country. In contrast, the trademarks we are working on today will more often be seen on mobile devices, in animation, and as website browser icons.

In recent years, the graphic design profession has been transformed by innovation. Advances in computer software offer near infinite possibilities for exceptionally precise rendering and speedy execution. Not only have our design tools evolved, but the entire media landscape has also radically changed. With today's incredibly fast access to communication of all sorts, people are constantly surrounded by ephemeral imagery. In this supersaturated visual environment, the essential characteristic of effective trademark design—to endure over time and thus fix an identity in the mind of the public—is even more meaningful for a company or institution.

While the world has changed, our basic approach to trademark design has not.

In *Identify*, we demonstrate our problem-solving approach to identity design. While it is an essentially creative process, we do not follow any personal artistic agenda or style. Instead, we work in the service of clients and address the challenges and parameters they bring to us in their search for a visual identity. We call these parameters "the design problem."

Typical design problems may be: the current trademark is too complex in form (as was the case with NBC), or the current trademark is no longer relevant to a company's brand positioning (as was the case with Mobil Oil). Other design problems may be that a consistent identity system is needed to tie together various divisions, departments, or sub-brands (as was the case with the Smithsonian Institution) or that an identity doesn't work well in advertising (as was the case with Armani Exchange). Since more than one parameter is usually at play, every client's design problem is unique.

A good solution cannot be devised without fully understanding the problem. We therefore start every identity project by acting as a "sponge," trying to absorb as much relevant information as possible about the client. We want to know what distinguishes them from peers in their field, where they are going in the future, and what, from their perspective, the visual identity must help achieve. We review existing communications and branded materials and interview key personnel in charge of strategy and communications.

Once we feel we have defined the problem adequately and gained sufficient knowledge of the client and of the industry or field in which they operate, we begin to work out our strategy for designing an effective identity. One of the first questions we ask ourselves is whether the client and their design problem will require a symbol (an icon or graphic image that appears with the name) or simply a memorable typographic treatment of the name (called a "wordmark" or "logotype").

Short, distinctive names are often enough by themselves to identify an entity, as they did for Xerox and Dime. A symbol can help unite subdivisions under a single visual identity system, as it did for Merck Pharmaceuticals. A symbol can also work as a decorative visual shorthand that embodies the brand, as was the case for the Korean department store Shinsegae. In considering these questions, we begin to define the logical parameters of the eventual solution, which lays the ground for the creative work to come.

This is where the science—which is everything we learned in the previous phase and the strategy that grows from it—meets the art, which is the intuitive exploration of conceptual design solutions. In this phase, thoughts and feelings take form.

We sketch our ideas by hand—using pencils, pens, china markers, or paint brushes and often correction fluid, rulers, and compasses. We sketch on paper or tracing paper, sometimes tearing it or cutting it with scissors. The rough designs are then scanned and translated into digital artwork. This process includes a great deal of tweaking by hand: we print the designs, trace them, rework them by hand, scan them again, and so on.

Sketching by hand gives a designer an immediacy of artistic expression and intuitive extension of creative impulses that as of now using the computer lacks. We are looking for the most direct connection between an idea and the creation of a form. In the early conceptual phase, the computer's preprogrammed functions often just get in the way.

Although each of us develops his own sketches, we work collaboratively, constantly looking over one another's shoulders, asking questions, making suggestions, and offering alternatives. As a result, the concepts improve and become stronger very quickly. We eventually pin up our designs and sit together to review, critique, and identify the most promising directions to be carried further.

How do we judge the designs? Identity design is not about what one likes or dislikes. It's about what works. Personal preferences for colors, shapes, or styles do not prevail. Therefore, we judge each of our early design concepts by the following criteria: Is it appropriate? Is it simple? Is it memorable? These terms can mean many things in different contexts. Here's what they mean to us:

By appropriate we mean that the trademark is relevant in form and concept to the client and its field or industry. For example, if the client's industry is fashion, the mark may need to be elegant. If the client is in the sports industry, the mark may need to be bold and dynamic. We say appropriate, but not necessarily expressive. Although sometimes we have an opportunity to create a mark that conveys literal ideas about the entity represented (such as for the Library of Congress and PBS), more often than not, a trademark cannot express a great deal in detail. We often speak of a successful trademark as a vessel that can hold the associations relevant to the company or organization rather than actually illustrate them. This is because of the next criterion: a trademark has to be simple.

By simple we mean that a trademark has to be focused in concept—have a single "story"—and, in most cases, must be uncomplicated in form. This is so it can work effectively and flexibly in a wide range of sizes and media—in small size on a business card, in different physical materials such as those used for signage, and in pixels in the digital realm—even as a website browser icon. But the simplicity of the mark is only valuable as long as the third criterion is met: a trademark must be memorable.

By memorable we mean that while the form must be simple, it must also be distinctive—unusual enough to be remembered. Of course, the simpler the form is, the less special it tends to become. And so our practice often explores the continuum between simple and distinctive. In other words, how memorable can the design be while remaining simple? How distinctive can we make the mark while keeping it focused? You can sometimes tell that the right balance has been struck when, after a brief time of looking at a mark, you can easily draw it from memory.

Adherence to these criteria can produce marks that have the potential to endure: they are relevant to the client and can be used flexibly and consistently, so they don't need to be changed in the foreseeable future. They can be simple enough to read in an instant and memorable enough to persist in one's mind. Based on these three criteria, therefore, we select the most promising design alternatives—almost always more than one, because there is rarely a single right answer.

Getting ideas from the sketch pad to the public eye requires careful and rigorous testing. Unlike other communications disciplines, such as advertising or marketing, in which testing verbal or visual messages by market survey or focus group can provide valuable input, trademark design requires considerations other than immediate, subjective reactions. In other words, when people see a completely new form, they might say things like: "I don't like blue" or "Squares are boring" or "It reminds me of some other thing." It is only after a mark is officially adopted that the public will embrace it and with time come to associate it with their feelings about the company or institution it represents. Like a good red wine, a trademark needs to mature, so evaluating it in concept form requires the judgment of an expert versed in assessing functionality.

Applying the designs to communications relevant to the client, such as stationery, publications, website identification, signage, or mobile-device apps, allows us to judge which concepts are the most effective in identifying the entity consistently. As we apply the design concepts, we develop a distinctive color palette and typographic style—a complete visual language that complements and helps accentuate the trademark designs.

We share with the clients only the solutions that can work effectively for them. We present these design alternatives shown in applications. In conversation with the client, who knows their own field best, we review the advantages and disadvantages of every solution and arrive together at a preferred design.

Each of the following trademarks was the result of the disciplined but creatively open process described here. All were presented to and ultimately adopted by the client. The approach practiced in these cases can produce trademarks that achieve an enduring level of public awareness—indeed, that can become iconic. We hope that *Identify* helps make this process more widely understood.

Although the trademarks in this book are arranged in no particular order, some thematic or methodological connections can be found. We discuss the design process more fully in the cases that represent different aspects of our approach to identity design.

The **Library of Congress** is the largest library in the world and the United States' oldest federal cultural institution. Since its founding in 1800, the Library has grown into a complex organization serving multiple constituencies. It also includes the research arm of Congress, the U.S. Copyright Office, the American Folklife Center, an extensive Braille library, and other specialized divisions. By 2008, the Library had developed dozens of individual graphic representations for those various divisions.

After an internal brand strategy process, which was driven in large part by a desire to increase public awareness of the Library and its free public resources, the Library turned to us. The Library wanted a new graphic identity that would ensure "thinking, communicating and behaving as one enterprise connected by a unified vision." Extensive interviews with stakeholders and an audit of past identification schemes for the Library's constituent parts further underscored the need to harmonize the organization's image.

To achieve this goal, we believed a symbol was needed. And in fact, the Library already had a history of identifying itself with symbols based on the dome of the Library's historic Jefferson Building.

But there were a number of problems with using the Jefferson Building dome as the basis for a symbol for the entire Library. For one thing, this domed building sits across the street from a much more famous dome—

that of the United States Capitol. (The Jefferson Building dome was once gilt, but since the decision in 1931 to remove the gold leaf and allow the copper to acquire its current patina, the Capitol dome has maintained its dominance over the landscape of Washington, D.C.) Also, the shape of the dome looked like a food tray cover and was hard to recognize visually. And more importantly the dome said nothing about what the Library did or what it was all about; as a symbol, it merely said that the Library occupied a building with a dome on top.

We saw an opportunity to ditch the dome altogether and create instead a one-of-a-kind mark that carried a rich set of meanings for the Library and its myriad divisions, programs, and activities.

The solution that we came up with was a combination of an allusion to a library and a representation of the American nation: an open book and the American flag. This is a clear distillation of the core identity of the Library of Congress as the national library of the United States, and it's hard to think of any other organization for which this symbol would be appropriate.

The curves of the open pages were rendered to suggest other symbolic associations, namely life, motion, knowledge, and information flowing from a central core. The idea of a book is general enough to apply across the Library's many services and departments, which are also suggested by the stripes.

The Library of Congress has had various identifying marks, as shown below. The new trademark symbolizes the institution's role as the national library, an improvement on the depiction of the dome of the Jefferson Building that had been used in the past.

Another key part of the identity was a new wordmark. Chermayeff & Geismar recommended dropping the opening "The"—which we discovered was never an official part of the Library's name—so that the words "Library of Congress" could be stacked as a fully justified unit to add distinction. We chose the typeface Trajan, inspired by the monumental lettering over the entrance to the Library's Great Hall and the classic inscriptions in Rome that mark what some say is the site of that city's great ancient libraries.

Even the greatest of libraries must periodically renew itself to remain useful to the general public. As the Library of Congress attempts to broaden its appeal at a time when the internet is fast becoming the primary source of public information, the new identity can take it beyond the physical building in which it is housed.

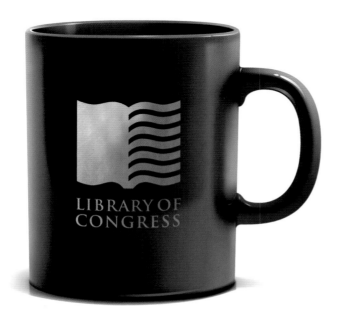

The symbol and wordmark are part of an extensive initiative to have various components of the Library speak in a unified voice through a consistent typographic style and the use of artistic photography featuring the spectacular art and architecture of the Jefferson Building.

LIBRARY OF
CONGRESS

It's More Than
a Library

By the time the **National Broadcasting Company** hired us in 1980, it had run into serious difficulties with its visual identity. In 1975, NBC had introduced a stylized letter *N* logo: bright, bold, and modern. But as NBC discovered to its horror, the trapezoidal design had already been trademarked by the Nebraska ETV Network. NBC ended up paying the Nebraskan network a substantial sum of money to abandon the design and transfer the rights to NBC.

However expensive and embarrassing obtaining the *N* had been, the identifier by which many people recognized NBC was the old peacock logo, which had been initially introduced in 1956 as a promotional image for color television. So in 1979, NBC decided to bring back the old peacock and superimpose it on an outline of the 1975 *N*.

Not only was this hybrid a busy and rather confusing image, it also didn't work very well as a corporate logo in various sizes and media. The peacock's feathers were small and required careful, expensive printing for even the simplest tasks, not to mention the challenges to legibility on the screen for a major television network.

The first decision we made was to get rid of the *N*. Although it had cost the network so much money and caused so much grief, it seemed completely wrong to highlight the first initial of the three-letter designation NBC, which was how everybody knew the network.

The peacock was a different story. Although in reality the peacock is a mean, nasty bird with a terrible temper, it was certainly an icon that indicated color and, by extension, color television. It also had built quite a bit of equity over the years as a representative of NBC. For these reasons, we felt that the peacock concept should be retained.

However, the rendition of the old peacock was unusable. We had to reimagine the form to make it effective. We streamlined the bird's outline, reduced the number of feathers to six, and regularized their shape. The bright colors assigned to the feathers are the primary and secondary colors of television. The peacock had been facing left—the wrong way for a reader's eye—so we flipped it to face right. Finally, we redrew the peacock so that the bird's body becomes, essentially, an upside-down feather, created in the negative space. All of these details helped make the peacock less of an illustration and more of a symbol.

The shape of the pointed *N* from 1975 is recalled in the simple letterforms we designed for the NBC name, which generally appears under the bird. Finally, a comprehensive set of guidelines putting forth rules for the proper use of the logo was developed.

At the end of this process, which was one of the most involved redesign efforts we've ever taken on, we were astonished to learn that NBC was not actually ready to adopt the new identity—not just yet. At the time, NBC was third in the rankings, behind ABC and CBS. The company was reluctant to undertake the expense of changing its signs, trucks, promotions, and so on until it was officially number one. It wasn't until 1986, six long years after NBC first hired us, that the network took the number-one slot and the new peacock was released into the world. It has since become one of the world's most recognized trademarks.

1956

1975

1979

1980

The evolution of the NBC trademark.

Pages from the extensive design manual (above) and the stationery system (facing page) hint at the scope of this program and at the flexibility of the simple peacock design.

MEMO

NBC
SPORTS

NBC
ENTERPRISES

Date

From

To

Date

From

30 Rockefeller Plaza
New York, NY 10020
212 664 4444

NBC
RADIO

National
Broadcasting
Company, Inc.

Date

NBC

NBC
TV STATIONS

Date

From

To

NBC
ENTERTAINMENT

112 West Center
Fayetteville, AR 72701
501 443 2400

Date

From

To

KPOM-TV
4624 Kelley Highway
P.O. Box 1867
Fort Smith, AR 72902
501 785 2400

24
KPOM-TV
FORT SMITH

NBC
TV NETWORK

Date

From

To

The simplicity of the peacock symbol allows it to be used in a wide variety of forms, from various broadcast applications to cut bronze metal shapes at the entrance to NBC's Rockefeller Center studios.

Below are a few early sketches for the peacock design.

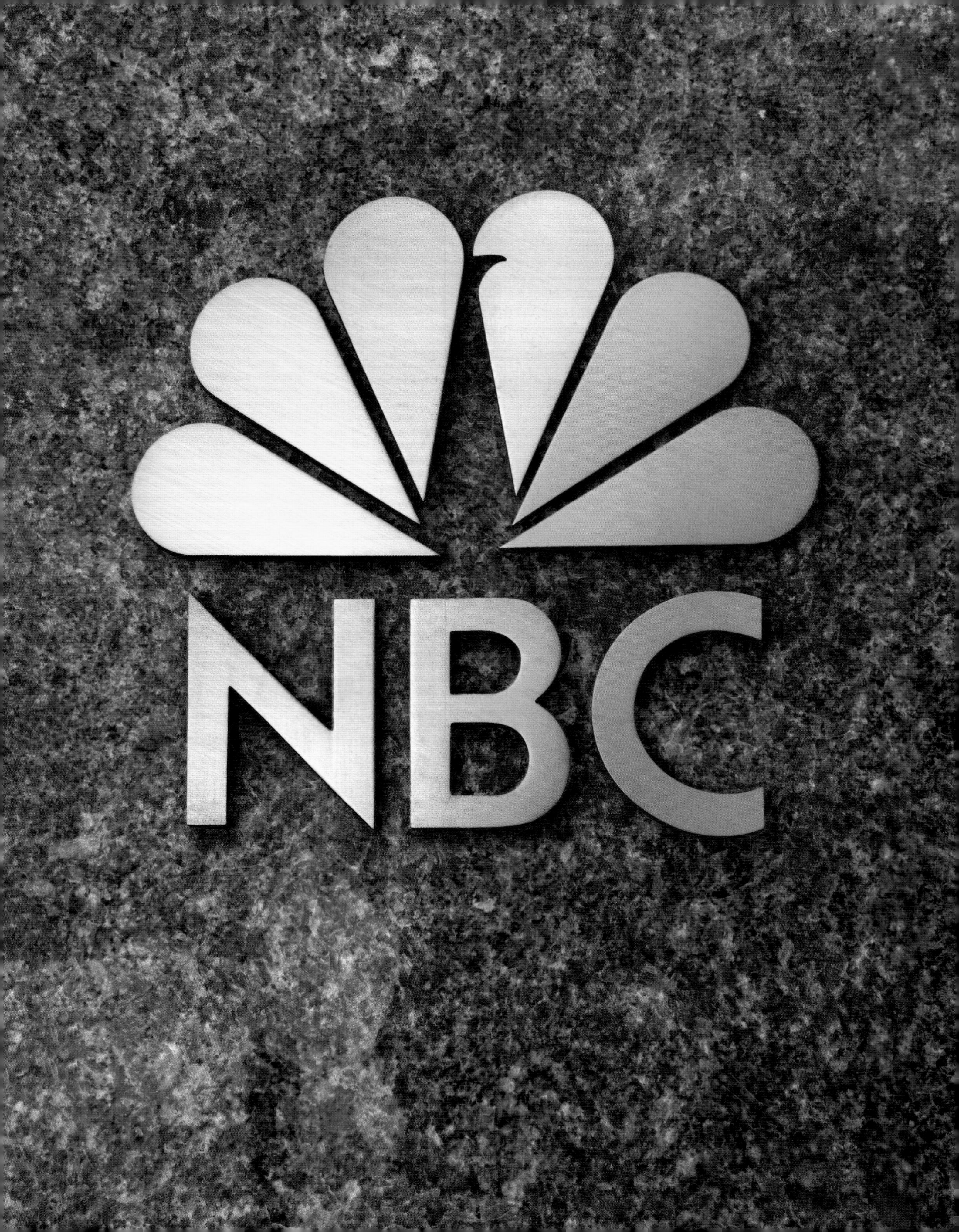
NBC

The fashion brand **Armani Exchange** had a challenge: The letters *A* and *X* with a vertical slash between them, which had gained so much recognition since the brand's launch in 1991, had never been conceived as a logo. The elements were too light and disjointed to make an impact, especially when used with provocative photography in print and online media advertising.

Tom Jarrold and Matthew Scrivens, the directors of advertising and branding at the company, came to Chermayeff & Geismar in 2008 and asked us to look at this problem, which they had tried to deal with internally for years. But what do you do with a mark that already has so much brand equity and yet has insufficient visual impact?

Jarrold and Scrivens at Armani Exchange gave us free rein to explore and recommend a new mark. We resisted the temptation to create something completely new, even though that meant that our design work in this case might go unnoticed. We realized that the brand equity was too valuable to jettison on a whim. Instead, we made a series of precision tweaks that solved every aspect of the problem.

We proposed the following: to make the A|X identity stand out better against strong advertising images, we reversed the letters out of two identical rectangles. The small gap between the rectangles recalls the thin line separating the *A* and *X* in the old design, and the two boxes recall military dog tags—a nice visual reference for a brand whose origins are in military exchange stores.

We also drew new letterforms based on the classic Didot typeface used for the rest of the Armani brand family. The bold strokes of the *A* and the *X* were made parallel to visually unify the two letters.

Jarrold and Scrivens agreed with our recommendations and appreciated our preservation of the brand equity that had built up with these initials over the years. Before our solution could be officially adopted, though, it had to pass one more test: Giorgio Armani in Milan had to approve it.

When Armani was first shown the redesign, he rejected it outright. However, we found out that due to his infamously busy schedule, the new mark had been presented to him between meetings, on a white piece of paper. The A|X directors then suggested approaching him a second time (which they almost never do) with our entire presentation, showing the logo in such applications as magazine ads, storefronts, and billboards. Once he saw the increased visual impact of the new identity in context, Armani immediately approved it.

The updated A|X logo is a bolder, visually stronger mark that now holds its own in an advertising context, without any loss of brand recognition. The new mark also functions as a self-contained icon that works better in the small sizes needed for clothing labels. Just as important: the world still recognizes it.

Making the bold strokes of the *A* and *X* parallel and superimposing them onto two rectangles made this iconic abbreviation visually bolder and more cohesive.

The visual weakness of the original A|X mark made it difficult to use in advertising. The revised mark, shown here in recent advertisements, is both strong and elegant.

The Solow Building at **9 West 57th Street** is a major office building in midtown Manhattan, rising above the surrounding buildings just south of Central Park with a striking ski-slope façade. In 1979, developer Sheldon H. Solow asked us to design the identity for his distinguished building, designed by Gordon Bunshaft of Skidmore, Owings & Merrill.

He was expecting a street number for the façade with a trademark, perhaps and a primary-color palette. This is the sort of visual identity other major buildings have.

What we came up with turned an identity into public art. In lieu of a number for the façade, we designed a massive, nine-foot-high, sculptural numeral 9 to be placed on the sidewalk, right in the flow of pedestrian traffic.

How do you introduce a client to an idea that so completely exceeds your mandate? That required another bold move.

We prepared an unconventional presentation for our proposal. At the time Solow had an office in the Seagram Building with floor-to-ceiling glass walls, and it became clear that our small model would be seen against the city outside. For scale and contrast, it also seemed like a good idea to present the idea to Mr. Solow on a rainy day. The rain made the streetscape in the window appear gray, a backdrop against which the red number 9 seemed all the more vibrant and eye-catching. To arrange this required patience (and the compliance of his secretary) as we waited for the rain.

We set up a small street scene on his wide windowsill, with photo cutouts from old magazines of people with umbrellas in the rain to go with the raindrops outside and on the Seagram's windows. All this was waiting for Mr. Solow when he returned from lunch.

Faced with this display, Solow approved our unexpected proposal.

Implementing this monumental number was next. The 9 is made from half-inch-thick steel plate and weighs 3,000 pounds, necessitating a steel supporting column that runs through three floors of underground garage. And the actual space that the 9 occupies is public property and had to be leased from the city for an annual charge. Since the sculpture is directly in the sidewalk, we chose a hard paint veneer to cover it; still, the diamond rings of passersby leave scratches in the paint. To keep the color fresh, the 9 is repainted several times a year.

By exceeding our mandate, we made our job more challenging. But the result is a bold, memorable marker for the building that does far more than identify the address. The 9 has taken on a life beyond the sidewalk. It was incorporated, along with its signature red color, into a logotype for the Solow Building Company. Later, a restaurant opened in the building's below-ground floor, taking the name "8 1/2." The 9 has become a New York City attraction, and, having appeared in films like *Superman* and television shows like *Sex and the City*, it has taken a place in popular culture as an American landmark.

SOLO9W57

The giant sculptural figure nine in front of the Solow Building on West 57th Street was put on city property directly in the path of pedestrians. It has become an iconic landmark of New York City, often appearing in film and television.

When building owner Sheldon H. Solow opened a restaurant in the lower level, he named it 8 1/2 because of the fame of the red 9 upstairs at street level.

8½

As with the large red nine, seemingly bold numbers and letters can form effective identifiers. **WGBH** is public television in Boston and **Channel 2** its local station. The logotypes for both were designed with double shadows, and the channel number was designed to take an actual three-dimensional form whenever possible. The sketches below right are from the presentation of this concept to WGBH. The design team at WGBH developed many imaginative iterations of the idea, including the "2-mobile" that toured the state to raise funds and the neonlike animation of the WGBH name that serves as a sign-off for the programs the station produces.

When Chase National Bank merged with the Bank of the Manhattan Company to create **Chase Manhattan Bank** in 1955, the new company became the largest commercial bank in New York and the second largest in the United States. The new organization needed a new graphic identity to represent it effectively. The plan was to launch the new identity together with the opening of the new headquarters building, a 60-story skyscraper then under construction in Lower Manhattan.

Banks at that time generally used trademarks that grew from their initials or an image of the bank's headquarters building. Chase Manhattan briefly used an awkward combination of a map of the United States, a representation of the globe, the name of the bank, and the phrase "world-wide banking."

We became convinced that the bank would benefit from a simple symbol that could not only unite the two newly merged corporate cultures but also come to stand in for the company's unwieldy name in the public mind.

However, there is no symbol that really means banking, and no symbol that represented Chase. The new headquarters building was large and rectangular, not easily distinguished from similar skyscrapers, so we could not base a symbol on the shape of the headquarters either.

We turned to the idea of an abstract symbol, since we knew that Chase Manhattan had tremendous advertising resources that could quickly establish the symbol in the public mind.

The blue octagonal mark is abstract but not without meaning. It suggests a Chinese coin or, with the square enclosed in an octagon, a bank vault and by extension the notion of security and trust. The 45-degree angles give the mark motion and dynamism, even a hint of three-dimensionality, yet it remains quite simple.

The presentation to the Chase Manhattan top executive board that would decide on the new symbol was quite dramatic. Two of the three top executives resisted the very idea of an abstract symbol, which wasn't surprising—at the time, no major American company used an abstract symbol to identify itself.

The executives then tried to brainstorm figurative design solutions. The company had recently commissioned sculptures for its new headquarters. Perhaps, one of the executives proposed, one of these sculptures could form the base of the corporate mark? The works of the sculptors in question—Alexander Calder, Alberto Giacometti, and Jean Dubuffet—would have made for an interesting, if odd, mark for a major bank. We had to explain the problems with that approach rather gently.

One of the top executives, David Rockefeller, who would soon become president and later chairman and CEO of the bank, was passionately interested in art, having come from a family tradition of art collectors. To our delight (and relief), he ultimately made the final call in favor of the octagonal symbol in 1960.

Within months, the same executives who had opposed the mark were proudly wearing it on cufflinks and tie tacks. It had rapidly become a corporate icon. We were almost astonished at how quickly and absolutely the executives had identified with the new mark. This experience has become an important touchstone for us: people can transfer their positive associations with a company onto even the most simple and abstract of designs, even if it's utterly foreign at first.

Previous trademark

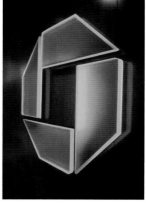

Because of various mergers and acquisitions in the past few decades, Chase has had many owners. But throughout all the changes, the octagonal symbol, the color blue, and the Chase name have been retained.

The photo at left shows the original entrance to Chase Manhattan Plaza in 1961. The photo above shows the trademark in a current, more flashy iteration.

Preliminary sketches for the Chase symbol (below left).

The simplicity of the symbol allows it to be rendered in a range of materials and forms. The three-dimensional version of the symbol shown at the right was designed for a prestigious branch on Park Avenue. Here, the dimensional forms themselves define the mark.

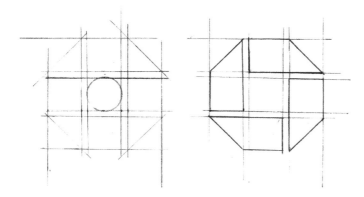

In 2010, Israeli entrepreneurs Ami Ben David and Rami Kasterstein were getting ready to launch a new search engine to challenge Google's market dominance.

The new engine, called **Do@**, offered a new search experience. When a user typed in a query, instead of generating a list of links to external URLs, the engine would display results in the form of iPhone apps, in which the user could do things (buy a book, watch a video, read a Wikipedia article) right at the Do@ site—hence the name.

But this short, well-chosen name nevertheless posed a serious problem. More than any other client we've had, Do@'s exclusive area of operation was the web, and yet one of the three characters in the name—the @ symbol—could not be used for its URL. The company secured the next best possible domain name, www.doat.com, an address that, although short and sweet, reads as an irrelevant and awkward word: *doat*.

This dilemma had to be solved before the search engine could go live, which is where we came in.

In the case of Do@, there were no alternatives. As soon as we came up with the following design solution, we knew that there could not be a second, equally successful option. We took the two identifiers—"Do@" and "doat"—and combined them visually. We thereby created a new typographic character: an @-like symbol that includes a T. This form ensured that people would immediately read the name as intended (Do@) but then, with the secondary discovery of the T, would clearly understand the domain name. Just as important, the design guided the reading of the URL as two words: *do* and *at*.

The Do@ identifier had to allow for a shorthand that could be used as an iPhone app icon.

do@at

A long working relationship with Ivan's brother Peter Chermayeff, one of the leading aquarium architects in the world, has resulted in our being involved with numerous aquarium projects in many countries. Our first aquarium project in 1968 was the identity and murals for the **New England Aquarium** in Boston. Later, we also designed identities and exhibition art for the **National Aquarium in Baltimore**, the **Osaka Aquarium Kaiyukan** in Japan, the **Tennessee Aquarium** in Chattanooga, as well as the **Oceanário de Lisboa** in Portugal. These projects have given us a chance to learn a great deal about marine life, but they have also provided a great design challenge: how to find new ways to represent similar institutions.

Aside from the obvious emphasis on sea life, Peter Chermayeff articulated a very clear, distinct concept for each of these projects; in that sense, the underlying themes vary considerably.

This focus on the specific role of each aquarium helped us to avoid repetition in the marks. Since the basic concept of the symbol always had to be marine life, we tried to emphasize what was particular and unique to each institution. For example, the National Aquarium in Baltimore is about fish and the water that covers over 70 percent of our planet. Therefore, the symbol we designed features the forms of fish interwoven into waves.

On the other hand, the Tennessee Aquarium focuses on the incredible aquatic and animal life around the Tennessee River and its tributaries, so the mark represents various species interlocked around a meandering waterway.

Drawing on similar imagery for inspiration, the symbols, when seen together, seem to bear a family resemblance. However, not only is each symbol tied to a particular idea about a particular place, but, in fact, these marks are never presented together out in the world where they function. (After all, the aquarium in Tennessee is not really competing with the aquarium in Osaka.)

Each one of these projects represented for us a vast learning experience about a particular aspect of the marine world. Our methodology requires in-depth investigation into the fields of each one of our clients as the first step in every identity design process. These aquarium projects exemplify one of the less talked-about perks of being identity designers: we get to go to school every day, and there's no tuition involved.

Aquariums are among the world's best-attended public attractions, providing seemingly endless fascination for many millions of people. The challenge for the identity designer is to find and to emphasize the characteristics that make each aquarium special.

← Exhibits
Information
Restaurant

The **National Aquarium in Baltimore** emphasizes both animal life and the water that covers our planet. To convey this idea, a figure-ground pattern of fish and waves was designed as a mark and as a repeat pattern for other uses.

The huge serrated walls in the entrance lobby convey one image to entering visitors and a completely different image to those exiting.

The **Tennessee Aquarium** in Chattanooga features the fish and bird life of the Tennessee River and its tributaries. The colorful symbol conveys many aspects of this concept, with the winding river formed by the shapes of the wildlife.

For the interior ceiling we developed a pattern of continually flowing light to let the visitors feel as though they were underwater themselves.

At the **Osaka Aquarium Kaiyukan**, in Japan, the symbol conveys the aquarium's focus on the Ring of Fire, the series of moving tectonic plates that surround the Pacific Ocean and are the site of most major earthquakes.

We developed a tile mural for the exterior walls of the aquarium, which open onto a giant plaza. The installation took 10 days. The 1,000s of tiles involved required each of the 12 installers to keep a detailed notebook.

The symbol for the **Oceanário de Lisboa** conveys a school of fish, with the eyes doubling as bubbles in the water.

For the many solid walls of the building, we designed a series of murals depicting specimens of aquatic life in the aquarium. Traditional Portuguese tile patterns were sorted in 10 degrees of blue—from solid blue to white—which we designed in geometric forms. The murals were then created according to the same percentage of density found in pixelated black-and-white marine photographs. The various images required 34,000 tiles.

The **New England Aquarium** in Boston was our first aquarium project, and it was one of the first truly modern aquariums. The trademark is equally modern in its bold simplicity.

A team from **Showtime Networks**, headed by then communications director Len Fogge, came to us in 1997 for a new graphic identity. The company's previous mark was a logotype that was bold, but not particularly memorable. "Showtime" is a generic term—a description, not a unique name. We were therefore convinced that we needed to make the word visually special.

In newspaper listings and TV guides, each station appears as a three-letter code: CBS, NBC, HBO, and so on. The shorthand for Showtime in these listings has always been SHO. This abbreviation inspired our solution: we highlighted SHO in the name by shining a spotlight on it—a simple, appropriate metaphor for show business. And so the first three letterforms were reversed out of a perfect red circle.

Not only does the treatment instantly make the generic word unique, it also naturally produces a focused visual icon for use as on-screen channel identification. In fact, SHO is such an obvious abbreviation for "show" that we found that most people don't even realize that the *W* had fallen away.

Once the idea was right, the technical execution took a little fussing with. We had to get the spacing right, and, more important, the rendering of the contemporary lettering had to be very precise in order to complete the circle visually.

When we first approach a design problem, there is a certain level of mystery about the solution: we never know quite where we will come out on the other end. In this case, our solution went a step further than simply addressing the initial parameters—the requirement of making the generic name more distinctive—by creating a reminder and direct reference to the TV listing.

With the spotlight circle on SHO in Showtime, the pronunciation isn't altered, as the *W* is silent. The SHO abbreviation is also used in all newspaper broadcast listings.

Design Guidelines

2: Introduction

C...

All d...
Showtime's...
(including requests...
agencies or other outside...
to use Showtime Identity artwork...
should be referred to:

3: The Logotype

The keystone element of the Showtime identity is the Showtime Logotype. It is the common denominator in all visual communications throughout the organization and should be used on each visual manifestation. However, it should usually only be used once, in a prominent place, as repetition will erode the impact of the Logotype.

The Logotype is shown here in two versions, the Freestanding version and the Box version. These are shown in positive form in both black on white and red on white. The Logotype should always be in one color only. It is not permitted to split off the SHO part of the Logotype by using another color, for example, the Logotype must be all red, not red and black.

The Logotype should never be used in text or as part of a headline. When the Corporation, the Networks and the Networks' Franchises are identified in any headline or text, Showtime should be written in the same typeface and typographic treatment as the text itself.

No other words are to be added to the Logotype, except for official Networks, Franchises and Claim lock-ups as shown in Sections 6 and 7.

The letterforms in this Logotype have been carefully redrawn and spaced to give the work distinctive visual qualities of strength and elegance. Therefore the Logotype must never be redrawn, retraced, manipulated by computer or altered in any way. Camera ready artwork or digital artwork is available from the Creative/Marketing Services and must always be used for reproduction.

Freestanding Version

Box Version
Not for Corporate use

Design guidelines outline simple rules for using the Showtime trademark. In actual broadcast, the SHO mark is regularly used as channel identification.

At its vibrant and free-spirited Mexico City college campus, **Centro** provides a professional education in design, architecture, television, fashion, and marketing. When in 2010, Centro was looking to expand to new locations, we were asked to

reexamine the school's institutional identity. While the name Centro is short and memorable, it is also a generic word, literally meaning "center," which can get confusing. Wanting to keep the trademark straightforward and simple, as is appropriate for a

design school, we created a special treatment to convey the letter *E*, making the name visually distinctive. The reference to a capital *E* in a lineup of lowercase letters adds a whimsical touch, in keeping

centro

Founded in Des Moines, Iowa, in 1929, the **American Republic Insurance Company** weathered the Great Depression by staying small and carefully nurturing its honest reputation. In the early 1960s a new generation of executives began expanding American Republic's operations across the country, and Chermayeff & Geismar was asked to design an image that would function as a trademark for multiple advertising platforms while retaining a visual connection to the idea of the American heartland.

The company's early visual identity recalled the certificate vignettes widely used in the financial industry in the early 20th century: an image of the United States with the words *budget*, *planned*, and *security*, which radiated out to laurel wreaths and red sashes bearing the name of the company. An eagle perched over the entire image. This complex scene was difficult to use in large- or small-scale formats.

Abstract concepts like "insurance" are tricky to render visually. Also challenging was making a connection to the idea of America and at the same time creating an original mark. Our solution was to use two stars of the American flag and to transform one of the points in each to suggest an eagle shape, which harked back to the earlier identity. The two eagle/stars together, a smaller one nestled into the wing of the larger, suggest a protective relationship or the figures of a parent and child—two associations we thought perfect for a company known for its life insurance policies. The image was drawn as simply and cleanly as possible so that it would work effectively even in small sizes.

Given the flocks of eagle images used by American businesses, we knew that we had taken on a particularly difficult challenge: attempting to combine into a single distinctive image this often-used theme with the even more common motif of stars. However, uniting these forms within the idea of a parent and child and bringing these subjects into the realm most appropriate for this client ultimately turned it into a one-of-a-kind mark.

A mother eagle protecting its offspring is the symbol of American Republic Insurance. The symbol was fragmented for an annual report cover (left). Below: previous trademark.

The **Brennan Center for Justice** at New York University School of Law is a nonpartisan public-policy institute that focuses on fundamental issues of democracy and justice. To convey the emphasis on national concerns, the name of the organization is underlined in red—a reappropriation of the familiar stripes of the American flag.

BRENNAN
CENTER
FOR JUSTICE

"Calling All Men to Barney's" was a familiar refrain to generations of New Yorkers. It was the tagline used in radio commercials advertising the famous discount store for men's and boys' clothing at Seventh Avenue and Seventeenth Street.

In the mid-1970s, some 50 years after the store's founding by Barney Pressman, the family decided that it needed to get out of the discount business and become more fashionable. Over a period of years the store was handsomely renovated and expanded to more than 100,000 square feet of retail space. High-end women's clothing was then introduced, along with stylish housewares, cosmetics, and a chic restaurant. The newly elegant store and fashionable labels required a new graphic identity that was reflective of "Barney's" change in character. This is where we came into the picture, in 1981.

Clearly, a more elegant and adaptable trademark was needed. In looking at the possibilities, we found a series of wonderful typographic coincidences. We realized that, by adding "New York" to the name, we could have two equal lines of seven characters each. To do this we had to remove the apostrophe from the "Barney's" name, as well as take out the space between *New* and *York*. Removing the apostrophe turned the founder's inelegant first name into a vaguely Swedish-sounding, genteel family name, and the NewYork part read clearly, even without the space. Set in all capital letters, the two (or three) words formed a comfortable and elegant logo.

We also discovered that the *N* in *Barneys*, the middle letter, aligned vertically with the *Y* in *New York*. This came as a surprise to us, but it seemed like destiny once we noticed it. The hidden alignment was instrumental in selling the idea to Barney Pressman's son, Fred.

Arriving at this seemingly straightforward, cohesive arrangement required several subtle modifications. The spacing of the letters, the fineness of the letter stems, the width of the strokes—all these carefully considered alterations go practically unnoticed, but are essential to creating the poised, elegant, almost literary effect we wanted.

The Seventh Avenue building that housed the original store is now a museum, but **Barneys New York** has other luxurious locations across the country and overseas. With its simple, classy logotype leading the way, it is firmly ensconced as an exceedingly upscale retail establishment.

Dropping the apostrophe in "Barney's" allowed us to align the name with its home in New York. And when we did, we found NY in the middle of the two-line logotype, reading vertically.

BARNEYS
NEWYORK

Shopping bags, wrapping paper, and store awnings feature the distinctive two-line logotype to convey a sense of elegance appropriate to the offerings.

In the mid-1980s, the **Public Broadcasting Service** came to Chermayeff & Geismar for a visual identity that would help emphasize the "public" in public television.

The PBS logo at that time, designed by Herb Lubalin, recalled too much the three major television networks, which each also had three letters: CBS, NBC, ABC. But PBS is not a system or a network (the S stands for Service), and it is the individual stations that have their own identities and are responsible for fund-raising.

In order to make the point that PBS was a special case, we decided to move away from the three-letter logotype and to develop a symbol that could stand for the more inclusive concept of "public television."

In doing so, we recognized a rare opportunity to transform an element of the existing logotype into a symbol. Herb Lubalin's old logo had the P rendered as a human face in profile, which was referred to internally as "Everyman." We realized that this P could form the base of a new symbol. We flipped the face around (to read left to right) and gave it a gentle lobotomy. We then repeated the profile in both negative and positive form, to suggest a multitude, a public. We called this symbol, which has been the core of the PBS identity ever since, "Everyone." Our subtle homage to the man who created the original logotype is the typeface we designated for the PBS identity: Lubalin Graph.

Fourteen years later, PBS took the icon we designed a step further by placing it on a circular disc, thus protecting it further from background interference. We thought this was a great move. PBS has used the identity in a number of interesting ways over the years, and it has come to symbolize "public television" without overpowering the identities of the individual stations and their continued reliance on viewer contributions.

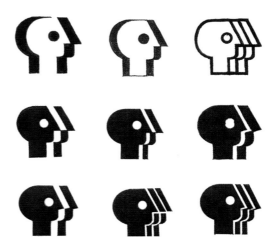

Previous trademark

PUBLIC
BROADCASTING
SERVICE

The P from the existing three-letter PBS logo, designed by Herb Lubalin, was turned to left to right, given a facelift, and expanded to become "Everyone," representing the idea of public television.

Above, early explorations leading to the final design.

Pages from the initial presentation and an animation storyboard suggest using the symbolic identity to emphasize the "public television" concept.

THE PUBLIC TELEVISION AUDIENCE 1983-4

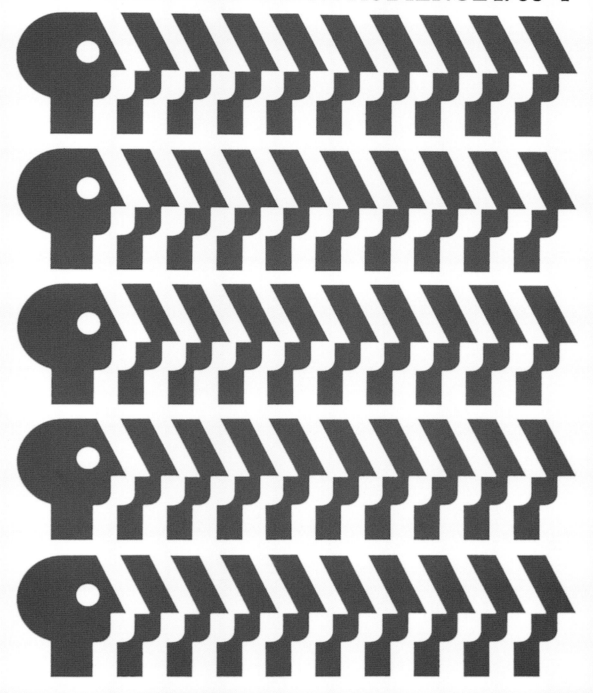

Half the Sky, a documentary series on PBS, focuses on the stories of women around the world who have overcome oppression and created opportunities for themselves and their communities.

The program was produced by Show of Force's Maro Chermayeff and Jeff Dupre. It is based on the book of the same title by Nicholas D. Kristof and Sheryl WuDunn.

The title comes from the Chinese proverb "Women hold up half the sky." The identity for the series suggests the image of the sky in two halves, creating the form of an equal sign.

half
the sky

The **Nippon Life Insurance Company** of Tokyo is one of the largest insurance companies in the world. Known as **Nissay** in Japan, Nippon Life has a long and respected history as a mutual insurance company, regularly paying dividends to its member policyholders since 1898. In 1989, Nissay looked to expand its marketing efforts beyond Japan's borders and realized that the classic Japanese seal it had used as an emblem was too limiting for an international company.

Nissay hired the branding consultant Motoo Nakamishi and his agency Paos to oversee a major strategic repositioning. Paos reached out to us when Nissay's need for an international and contemporary visual identity became clear.

Any company that has operated at such a scale and for so long has built up tremendous reputational equity, so it was important to preserve some continuity with the existing mark.

For such a simple mark, the Nissay boxed N required a great deal of experimentation. We developed a suite of alternative N letterforms, having decided in consultation with Nissay and Paos that a Latin character would convey a Western, international outlook. At the same time, we wanted to preserve something of the equity of the old mark by retaining the bright red color and, to a lesser extent, using an overall diamond shape.

The chosen N is active and directional. By placing the N in a box tilted on a diagonal, we created a symbol that pointed in all four cardinal directions, implying dynamism and expansiveness. At the same time, the box encloses the letterform, creating a minimal shape that refers back to the traditional geometric chop from which our mark is derived. The balance of shapes at the midpoint of the square conveys a sense of calm and security appropriate for an insurance company. With its Latin N, the mark is Western—but there's something undeniably Japanese about it as well—a balance that was not easily achieved.

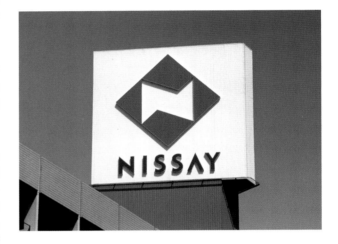

The giant Nippon Life Insurance Company (Nissay) was expanding internationally and felt that their very traditional mark (at left) was too limiting. The new identity retains the bold red color, but puts an abstract N in a dynamic form to convey a more international feeling.

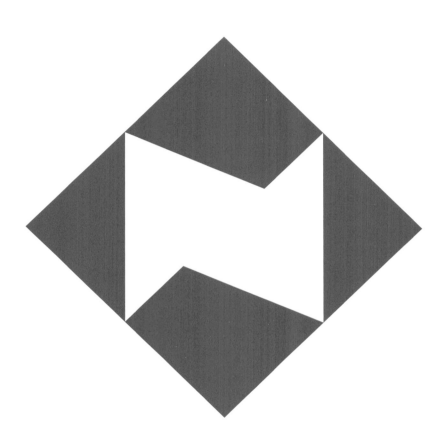

The **Turkish Leather Council**, a trade association with more than 400 members, needed a symbolic device to clearly distinguish genuine Turkish leather products from foreign imports. The symbol is inspired by an ancient design based on the skeletal structure of cattle.

A traditional motif also inspired the symbol we designed for the **Pera Museum** in Istanbul. The museum features permanent collections of Turkish Ottoman ceramics, weights and measures, orientalist painting, and temporary exhibitions of international contemporary art and photography. The stylized red design is based on a traditional rendering of a tulip indigenous to Turkey.

In 2009, **Conservation International** reached a seminal point in its history: they acknowledged that their traditional approach of protecting hotspots around the world for the sake of saving the environment had not worked. This leading environmental group then made a bold and revolutionary decision to change their mission and focus from protecting nature for nature's sake to protecting nature for the well-being of humanity. Their new strategy therefore would greatly expand their involvement into populated areas, such as cities and farmlands.

This strategic shift made their previous logo—an illustrative rendition of greenery with a primate hanging from a tree branch—irrelevant. The group's director of branding, Laura Bowling, came to us to create a new mark that would be appropriate for the new all-encompassing mission and that would set Conservation International apart from the many peer organizations dealing with environmental concerns.

We explored dozens of design concepts, including many that featured or were representations of a human figure. However, in the nonprofit arena the human figure has become clichéd. Throughout the sketching and exploration process, one simple concept rose to become our favorite: a blue circle underlined in green. Although the design was made of two simple, basic shapes, their combination and proportions did not look familiar. And it was appropriate: Bowling titled the form "our blue planet on a green path to sustainability."

Believing as we do in the principles of the modernist tradition, we constantly look for the ultimate simple form that can be expressive and memorable. Once the mark cleared the worldwide trademark legal search, we were convinced we had a winner.

However, our greatest challenge was still ahead. Convincing a client to follow your recommendation and adopt the design concept you deem best can be as great a challenge as actually creating the mark in the first place. This was the case with Conservation International.

The illustrative, highly complex mark Conservation International had had since its founding in 1971 was passionately beloved by almost every one of the organization's 900 employees, especially by the top echelon. We discovered that the primate hanging from the tree had in fact been hand drawn by the organization's president, a primatologist.

Furthermore, we came to realize that having lived with and loved the existing, highly illustrative mark, the decision makers found it extremely difficult to accept a simple, abstract form in its place.

In the ensuing months, we found ourselves honing our sales skills. We had to make the case that an effective mark can never express everything about an organization. Rather, a trademark is only a small part of an organization's communications, and its most important task is to be an effective identifier.

Early conceptual explorations are shown below. Left: previous trademark.

VIDEO BY THORNBERG & FORESTER

We assured the Conservation International leadership, based on our long experience, that a new, original mark would almost always seem foreign at first. For example, we talked to them about our initially challenging experience with Chase Bank in the 1960s. When our new visual identity was adopted, all the postive perceptions people had about the bank, as well as their feelings about it, were inevitably associated with the new mark.

Finally, we developed a short animated piece for Conservation International, paying homage to the old mark while transforming it into the new design. The sequence started with a monkey sitting in a tree, followed by an expansion of the camera view—suggesting the expansion of the scope of the organization's work—to other areas of conservation, including humans, and ended with the new trademark. With this animation, we were able to infuse the simple icon with passion, history, and rich meaning.

It was, finally, this animation that helped Conservation International begin to transfer their own positive feelings from the old mark to the new.

Together with motion graphics studio Thornberg & Forester, a brief video was developed to convey how the new identity reflects the broadening of the organization's mission. The poster on the facing page shows the emphasis on vibrant photography relating people and nature and the use of clean, simple typography.

people need nature to thrive

PHOTO COURTESY OF ART WOLFE

CONSERVATION
INTERNATIONAL

A wordmark featuring an underlined *M* identifies **El Mall**, a multimedia production company headed by media mogul Pedro Torres that is responsible for many of Latin America's most successful television shows. The emphasized *M* can be pulled out and used as a shorthand for the company when appropriate.

el mall

The **Alliance for Downtown New York** was formed in the early 1990s to manage the Downtown-Lower Manhattan Business Improvement District (BID) and to provide added security, sanitation, shuttle buses, way-finding, and street improvements to this famous historic area. After a year of operations, they recognized the need for a bold way to clearly identify their many physical and marketing efforts. In 1994, the Alliance asked Chermayeff & Geismar to consider the question.

It struck us immediately that the silhouettes of the two World Trade Center towers would work nicely as the two *L*s in the word *Alliance*, and we built a wordmark of a cityscape around that idea. That mark became well established all throughout the downtown district. In 1999, we modified the mark slightly to place the word-mark in a red square and to add the word "Downtown" to distinguish this organization from others that were being established in parts of the city.

Then came 9/11. Within a couple of days of the disaster, we got a call from the Downtown Alliance, asking us what should be done with the mark. The element that was the initial inspiration for the mark was now gone. For the immediate aftermath, the decision was to hold off making any dramatic changes.

Within a few months, however, it became clear that the wordmark needed to be changed. We redrew the two *L*s as two other typical but dissimilar downtown skyscrapers. While we made a few minor alterations to some other letters to make the new proportions work, in all important respects the mark did not change.

After 9/11, many companies that used the Twin Towers in their logo had a decision to make: some decided to keep the image, while others abandoned their marks altogether. We decided that the downtown district needed all the help moving forward that it could get. In this case, even though the substitution of two generic buildings for the wordmark took away from the original idea of the design, it was better to maintain continuity with a well-established mark than to have the towers become an issue that distracted from the Downtown Alliance's identity, as it surely would have.

1990

1999

2001

The symbol for the downtown Manhattan business district originally featured the Twin Towers of the World Trade Center as the two *L*s in "Alliance." After 9/11, the mark had to be updated, with those iconic towers replaced by more generic skyscrapers.

Downtown Alliance

1325 Avenue of the Americas
Open to the Public
8:00am to 7:00pm
Monday through Friday
Public access between
53rd and 54th streets

In the 1970s, midtown Manhattan
zoning was changed to encou-
rage developers to provide
spaces for the general public
within their high-rise buildings.
Known as **Public Spaces NYC**,
the tree-on-a-grid symbol was
developed to clearly identify
those locations that were often
not apparent from the street.

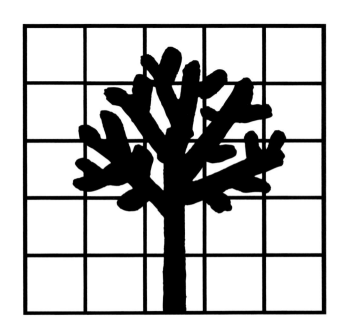

In 2003, the **Hearst Corporation** was moving out of offices dispersed all over New York City and into a shiny new glass tower on 57th Street, designed by Norman Foster. The company came to us to help make sure that its identity, which had been around since the 1950s, was ready to take a much more exposed place in the public eye. Hearst's existing mark was a somewhat complicated pictorial image of an eagle with striped wings.

As a media empire with numerous divisions, such as magazines, television stations, newspapers, and interactive media, the Hearst Corporation is essentially a parent company. It also needed a trademark that would work with all the existing trademarks of its various subsidiary brands. In other words, the new visual identity wouldn't have to brand the Hearst Corporation itself so much as proclaim Hearst's ownership of its many established media properties. For example, the Hearst identity would appear on the websites as well as on the spines of magazines such as *O, The Oprah Magazine*; *Esquire*; *Cosmopolitan*; *Marie Claire*; and *Redbook*, among many others—right alongside each magazine's own identity.

When we first contemplated the eagle symbol, exploring simplified versions of the existing rendition, it became apparent that it was a flawed proposition. There were two reasons to move away from the eagle.

For one thing, it's nearly impossible today to render a distinctive eagle. There are literally thousands of existing eagle trademarks currently in use. It's a classic American symbol and part of the Great Seal of the United States. Entities from Harley-Davidson to the U.S. Postal Service to American Airlines all use eagle symbols.

But more important, we recognized that the Hearst Corporation did not need a symbol at all—eagle or otherwise. Each of the subsidiary media had its own visual identity. The Hearst mark, appearing alongside these marks, should not compete with them for visual impact and attention, as a pictorial symbol would.

We therefore worked to present the name itself as a distinctive and appropriate wordmark. For the parent company name, we used very bold letterforms, but spaced them widely apart for a more memorable appearance. To complement this strong, sans-serif typography, the generic division names are set in a classic typeface—lowercase Garamond Italic. This provides contrast to the Hearst wordmark, and adds a lightness and elegance to the overall look of the identity system.

The Hearst wordmark is one of the simplest, most straightforward marks we have ever designed. The characteristics that were expressed in the eagle—strength, authority, boldness—are embodied in this purely typographic design in a simple and immediate way.

Previous trademark

HEARST

HEARST *newspapers*

HEARST *business media*

HEARST *magazines*

HEARST *real estate*

HEARST *broadcasting*

HEARST *interactive media*

HEARST *entertainment*

HEARST *communications*

HEARST *tower*

HEARST *television*

The Hearst identity system, using only a distinctive but straightforward typographic format, helps tie together the company's broad range of media components in a clear and elegant way. The reception area pictured above is at the company's new landmark building in Manhattan.

eping   **HEARST** *magazines*

han'sDay   **HEARST** *magazines*

£   **HEARST** *magazines*

lire   **HEARST** *magazines*

L E   **HEARST** *magazines*

OLITAN   **HEARST** *magazines*

RIVER   **HEARST** *magazines*

R   **HEARST** *magazines*

OOK   **HEARST** *magazines*

hics   **HEARST** *magazines*

teen   **HEARST** *magazines*

OLITAN   **HEARST** *magazines*

lire   **HEARST** *magazines*

£   **HEARST** *magazines*

han'sDay   **HEARST** *magazines*

RIVER   **HEARST** *magazines*

eping   **HEARST** *magazines*

R   **HEARST** *magazines*

hics   **HEARST** *magazines*

L E   **HEARST** *magazines*

When **The Museum of Modern Art** was extensively renovated and expanded in the 1960s, we developed a very simple typographic style for the museum name and related signage.

A colorful graphic device was also developed at that time. It featured basic geometric forms—the square, the triangle, and the circle—in repeat patterns and was used on banners to announce the openings of new exhibitions and to make the entrance more visible from Fifth Avenue.

The Museum of Modern Art

Mount Sinai

Using clear typographic treatments can be an appropriate direction for the graphic identity of an organization with a short, easily recognized name. Shown here are two examples.

Mount Sinai Medical Center is a major New York City facility. The blue square adds visual strength to the lightweight lettering.

CB Richard Ellis, now the largest commercial real estate firm, uses the shorthand CBRE. The very bold, horizontally extended letterforms stand out clearly on signs and in advertisements.

Factset Research Systems supplies highly sophisticated global economic and financial data to investment professionals. Since the Factset name is short and memorable and since the potential audience is limited, using a distinctive lettering style for the name seemed a logical approach for the company's identity. Using the trademark in a bold but carefully integrated way provides a clear family look.

FactSet Research Systems Annual Report 1998

FactSet Research
Leaders in Financial Inform...

FACTSET

2009 Report on Activities

Mac
for
and
Ins

MacArthur Award for Creative and Effective Institutions

2010 F
Helpi

Advancing Human Rights and International Justice

2009
Report on Activities

Working in Nations
in Transition

The John D. and Catherine T. MacArthur Foundation

MacArthur Foundation

The John D. and Catherine T. MacArthur Foundation

MacArthur Foundation

The John D. and Catherine T. MacArthur Foundation

MacArthur Foundation

Another straightforward typographic approach is the one developed for the **MacArthur Foundation** in Chicago. We recommended using the simpler two-word title rather than the long and more formal "John D. and Catherine T. MacArthur Foundation," and to always use green and blue—the colors of the sky and the earth—to reflect the foundation's support for causes beneficial to all mankind.

MacArthur
Foundation

Over the years, we have had a few opportunities to use design to help affect broader social trends. One of these opportunities came in 1963, during the height of the Cold War. At this time, a continuing series of cultural exchange exhibitions took place in the United States and the Soviet Union. The subjects of these exhibitions tended to be nonideological: medicine, music, or fine art, for example.

The United States Information Agency (USIA), a division of the Department of State, was responsible for U.S. participation. Through the American Institute of Graphic Arts (AIGA), Chermayeff & Geismar was retained to design a large-scale traveling exhibition on all aspects of American graphic arts. The exhibit itself featured thousands of artifacts, from advertising materials, book covers, and illustrations to record album covers, prints, and commercial packaging.

An identity for the exhibit, titled **"Graphic Arts USA,"** was needed for posters, catalog covers, souvenirs, and other display items. It was important that the identity embody the national aspect of this venture as well as the visual and artistic focus.

We decided that a design combining two seemingly unrelated ideas—a pen nib and the American flag—would best symbolize the exhibition theme. This image proved to be an effective icon, most notably on the banners outside of the exhibition hall marking the entrance where visitors lined up in the cold to wait for hours.

"Graphic Arts USA" turned out to be a great hit, traveling for a number of years within the U.S.S.R. before moving on to the Eastern Bloc. The Soviet authorities may not have foreseen the popular appeal that a graphic arts exhibit might hold. Because it showed images and artifacts from daily life in America, the display was effectively a window into Western culture—and Western commercialism. People lined up for many hours to get a glimpse of this forbidden world. In this respect, graphic art was like an undercover agent, sneaking into the country as art, having an immediate impact as popular culture, and having a long-term influence as social politics.

In Moscow, thousands of Russians waited in line to see the exhibition of American graphic arts.

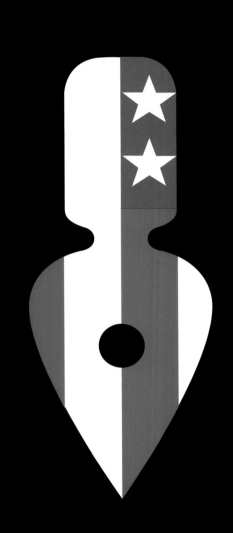

A portfolio of pieces by American graphic artists and illustrators was given to VIP visitors and other dignitaries.

The exhibit itself (facing page) focused on everyday materials in order to convey a sense of life in the United States.

John Fitzgerald Kennedy Library

Another national exhibition we designed was for the **John F. Kennedy Presidential Library** in Boston, which houses the documents and memorabilia of the president, as well as those of his younger brother, Robert F. Kennedy.

The trademark we designed to identify the library's communications, such as this publication cover (left), combines the famous initials so that they flow together and form a unified grouping.

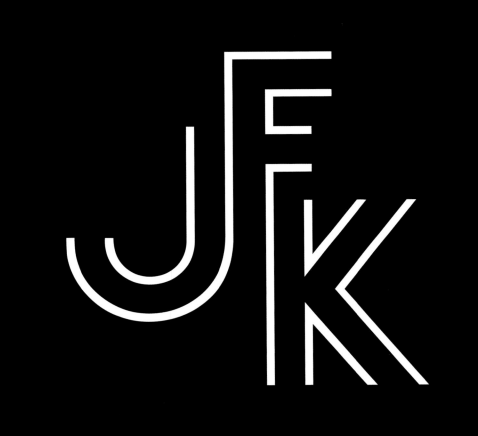

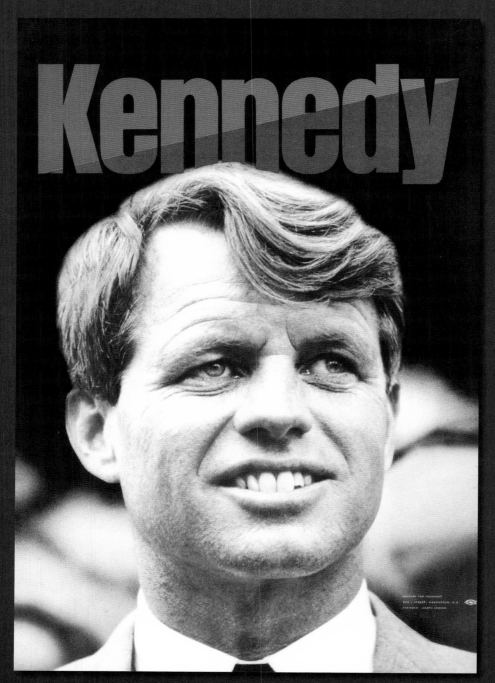

The Robert F. Kennedy Center for Justice and Human Rights was established in 1968, soon after his assassination. We were asked to design his initials to appear on the foundation's communications. Utilizing the white of the paper to represent the middle initial *F*, the mark appropriately uses a red, white, and blue color scheme.

We had developed the poster above for use in Robert F. Kennedy's 1968 presidential campaign. In recent years, this poster was adopted as the visual identity for the movie *Bobby*.

RFK

Founded by Billie Jean King in 1973, the **Women's Tennis Association** is the governing body for women's professional tennis worldwide. Despite the fact that tennis is the leading global sport for women, the WTA's name recognition had never been anywhere near equivalent to commensurate sports-governing bodies like the PGA, the NFL, or the NBA. This was largely due to the need to give naming rights to the major sponsor. What started as "The Virginia Slims Championship" years later became "The Sony Ericsson WTA Tour."

In 2010, the arrangement was changed, with Sony Ericsson as the lead global sponsor, but not the title sponsor. This change provided WTA the opportunity to reestablish its own core identity. With the new agreement in hand, WTA came to Chermayeff & Geismar to create a new trademark as the foundation for a newly invigorated brand.

Does a professional sports association logo have to feature a figure of an athlete playing that sport?

The most obvious conceptual direction for this identity was, indeed, to create a mark that communicates women plus tennis. The marks for other well-known professional sports organizations such as Major League Baseball or the National Basketball Association are based on this approach. When we conducted interviews with a group of representatives from the organization's important stakeholders, most felt that the new mark should express clearly women plus tennis.

We started off the exploratory phase with this notion and created a range of preliminary concepts that included figures of female tennis players, rendered in various styles and levels of abstraction. However, as the development process unfolded and we worked to test the various concepts we had developed, a strong and convincing case against the figure began to mount.

An obvious difficulty with the figurative-symbol approach is that the mark immediately has two elements—the wordmark and the symbol— rather than one, naturally giving less emphasis to each when space is restricted. For the WTA specifically, there was an added difficulty: a visual expression of a female tennis player is unavoidably a complex image, since certain details such as the racket and the hair are an absolute necessity for the symbol to communicate clearly. Such a complex form is harder to read in small sizes or when pixilated online or in broadcasting.

The most significant argument against the use of the figure in the mark was a strategic one: there was no need for it. The most frequent and important uses of the WTA identity are in context. Whether watching a match on the court or on television, visiting the WTA website or on a promotional communication (for one of the 50 tournaments worldwide), every time the audience is exposed to the WTA identity, it is always in clear and unmistakable connection to women's tennis.

Previous trademark

Sorana Cirstea

STRONG IS BEAUTIFUL

WTA

For these reasons, we ultimately recommended a simple but memorable typographic mark that put the emphasis squarely on the three-letter abbreviation. The design picks up on the common element in the three characters—that they are all composed of straight lines—and adds rounded edges to the strokes, giving the appearance of a path of a bouncing ball. The crossbar of the *A* is a circle, which, when consistently rendered in yellow, is a subtle but clear reference to tennis.

The ellipse shape that encases the letters is similar to that of a tennis racket and also to the ball mark shown in the Hawk-Eye replays. It adds boldness and visual impact, and "protects" the mark by ensuring color consistency and legibility on various backgrounds.

To our surprise and delight, it did not take much to convince the stakeholders to go along with our less orthodox recommendation. As brand-savvy clients, they immediately recognized the design limitations of the tennis-playing figure and were happy to embrace what is now an unusual mark in professional sports.

In one of a series of advertisements (above) that feature dramatic photography and a provocative statement, the WTA trademark holds its own without being overscaled. It also functions in a single color on stadium walls, as shown in presentation image at right.

Combat HIV/AIDS, Malaria and Other Diseases

Have halted by 2015, and begun to reverse, the spread of HIV/AIDS

Mobilizing for HIV/AIDS awareness: World AIDS Day, China

UN DP

The United Nations Development Programme (UNDP) is a large wing of the UN, charged with helping developing nations achieve sustainable human development. The program is generally referred to as UNDP in English speaking countries, but as PNUD in Spanish- and French-speaking areas. So the design challenge was to make a trademark using the initials that allows for two versions with a similar look. This was solved by putting the initials in four boxes, and featuring the UN symbol above them.

The poster shown at left is one of a series of 10 that focuses on the UN's Millennium Development Goals. Above is the Spanish and French trademark variant.

Initials can be used to make a single mark in certain instances— if they are well known.

General Fireproofing manufactured steel filing cabinets. But as the product line expanded, neither "general" nor "fireproofing" had any relevant meaning to the company's business.

Moreover, everyone referred to the company as "GF." So when the name was changed to **GF Business Equipment**, we developed an identifier based on the initials to help enforce the new name. The mark is an intriguing combination of positive and negative forms, with the white *F* actually defining the blue *G*.

The abbreviation for the **United States Environmental Protection Agency** is the EPA, and these initials are widely spoken and recognized. To take advantage of this fact, we developed a graphic identity that emphasized the initials and connected them to a simplified version of the seal that previously was the agency's only identification mark.

Owens-Illinois is one of the world's largest manufacturers of glass containers and plastic packaging. The hyphen allows the letter *O* of Owens and the letter *I* of Illinois to join each other memorably—a simple solution for a complex organization.

Rockefeller Center comprises 19 buildings on 22 acres in the heart of midtown Manhattan. But in spite of world-class name recognition, research revealed that few people had a clear (and correct) idea of what the Center actually is and how far it extends. As part of a major effort to upgrade and expand the facilities, Chermayeff & Geismar was asked to develop a new, unified visual identity to help clarify what Rockefeller Center is and to signal the extensive changes underway. The challenge was to develop a graphic identity that instantly said "new," but was at the same time respectful of and compatible with the Center's architecture and reputation.

The challenge in designing a mark was to find a contemporary way to incorporate various notions of the Center into a simple visual statement and to do so in a way that would seem absolutely appropriate to the Center, as if it had always been part of it.

The resulting identity is a combination of a symbol and a wordmark. The tall vertical lines of the symbol suggest

the architecture of the centerpiece GE Building, while the round form connotes the idea of the all-encompassing nature of the Center and its place in the heart of Manhattan. The overall geometric form and the even-weight lines reflect the Art Deco style of the architecture and related artworks.

For the second element of the identity, the name, a simple lettering style was selected, one that complements the geometry of the symbol and subtly reflects the age and style of this landmark.

The clarity and simplicity of the symbol and lettering have made them effective in a wide range of materials, from bronze and gold leaf on the buildings themselves to woven fabric and cast metal on uniformed personnel, from stitched nylon banners to mark the center's boundaries to print and digital promotion.

Today, Rockefeller Center has been cleaned up, modernized, re-gilded, and restored and is more clearly comprehended and understood within the crowded cityscape.

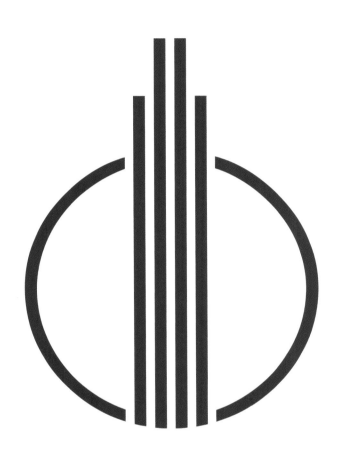

Banners march down the sidewalks of Manhattan's Sixth Avenue to mark the boundaries of Rockefeller Center and to reflect the Art Deco style for which it is famous.

The 30-foot-high inflated "cleaner" figure on the facing page was a temporary device we designed to call attention to the cleaning program for the exterior walls of all the Center's buildings.

The retail chain **Best Products** (1957–1997) offered the American consumer an unusual—and even avant-garde—shopping experience.

Called "catalogue show-rooms," the chain's warehouse-like stores displayed for customers one example of every product they sold. Each of the options for a particular product would be labeled "good," "better," or "best," from which, obviously, the company derived its name. If a customer wanted to purchase a particular model, he or she filled out a ticket, paid a cashier, and waited for the product to come down a chute from the upper-floor storage space.

It was what Best Products did to package this retail concept, however, that made the company so interesting.

The Virginian family that owned the stores, Sydney and Frances Lewis, were passionate collectors of contemporary art. (It was said that they would sometimes accept art in exchange for store credit.) In the 1970s they began making interesting buildings of their big-box stores—and made architectural history. They hired smart, cutting-edge architecture firms like SITE to create, in one case, a postapocalyptic façade, or, in another case, a giant terrarium. These strange and wonderful exteriors became visitor attractions themselves.

In 1979, the Lewises came to Chermayeff & Geismar to create a similarly playful visual identity. They were among those rare clients who gave us free rein to be experimental. Our logo had to work with the exciting, dynamic environments created by these wonderful architects.

What we came up with was a self-referential typographic logo that was a literalization of the company's name and business model: each letter larger than the preceding one, just as each product model was better than the last. On a sign, the letters themselves get thinner as they get taller, as though they were sinking under their own weight into the façade. We presented only a few variations of the same concept to the Lewises, as the idea seemed so unassailably right.

We feel privileged to have been part of this unique moment in postmodern design and architecture. The Lewises eagerly embraced artistic comment on their big-box stores, constantly taking chances with the consumer business model that had made them so successful. Such experimental and playful design was unusual for its time and, to our knowledge, hasn't been done since.

The wordmark appears to sink into the wall of this catalog showroom in Plantation, Florida. The SITE-designed building features a giant terrarium across the whole façade, with continual "rainfall" to keep the climbing vines growing.

BEST

Designing letters with a visual reference to the product is also the approach we took with **Kaya Group**, which makes ropes, harnesses, and strapping for the shipping, military, and construction industries of Turkey and Europe. These are marketed under many brand names. Based on an alphabet we designed to suggest the look of letters made from a single line of rope, the Kaya wordmark is a distinctive and meaningful identifier for the company's products and numerous industry-specific catalogs.

KAYA

Merck & Co. had been a major independent pharmaceutical company for almost a century when it came to us in 1991 for an identity overhaul.

A lot of the company's problems could be traced back to its coming-of-age trauma: founded in Darmstadt, Germany, in the 17th century, Merck had an American division that was seized by the U.S. Government in 1919. That meant that the American division became its own, independent company. There were now in the pharmaceutical world two competing companies named Merck. The American Merck is known in the European market as Merck, Sharp & Dohme (MSD). The German Merck is known in the North American market as EMD Chemicals. You can imagine the confusion.

Not only was the American Merck often confused with the German Merck, but Merck also had a number of major subsidiary companies. Merck's agricultural medicine division was known as MSD-ADVET. Then there were MCMD and Merck Pharmaceutical Manufacturing, and so forth. Each of these divisions had different unrelated visual identities.

So we were hired to help Merck—the American Merck, that is—come up with a cohesive identity that would better position the company within its market, strongly relating it to its European arm, MSD, while effectively differentiating it from the German company with the same name.

This case was a classic example of a challenge that called for symbol design; indeed our solution was to create a strong, simple icon to be used consistently across the company's divisions.

The symbol design itself suggests a multitude of appropriate ideas. It looks like a capsule overlaid with two smaller pills. The overall form is also reminiscent of a cross—a traditional marker for medical aid and pharmacies, and the basis for Merck's original visual identity. However, in its evocation of molecular compound diagrams, the mark's rounded symmetry is also very modern.

In the place of the dark green Merck had had, we recommended a bluer, lighter green, which is more distinctive and also appropriate to the medical field. But the lettering and the nomenclature still needed clarification. Together with a strategy consultant, we fixed each department's name into a standardized lockup, with MERCK in a bold logotype aligned with the mark, and the divisional name smaller and lighter beneath.

A symbol should never be a merely decorative element in an identity system. As in the case of Merck, an icon can be an irreplaceable tool for bringing together different divisions, companies, or entities with different names—even in different parts of the world. While there are other strategic reasons for using a symbol, there should always be some good reason for designing one.

Previous trademarks

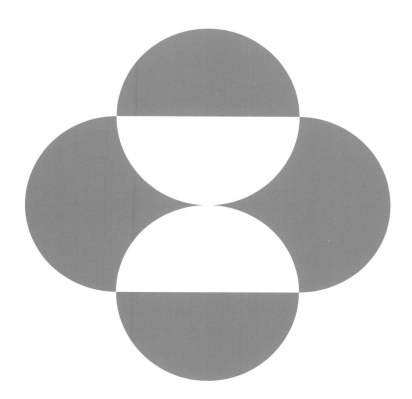

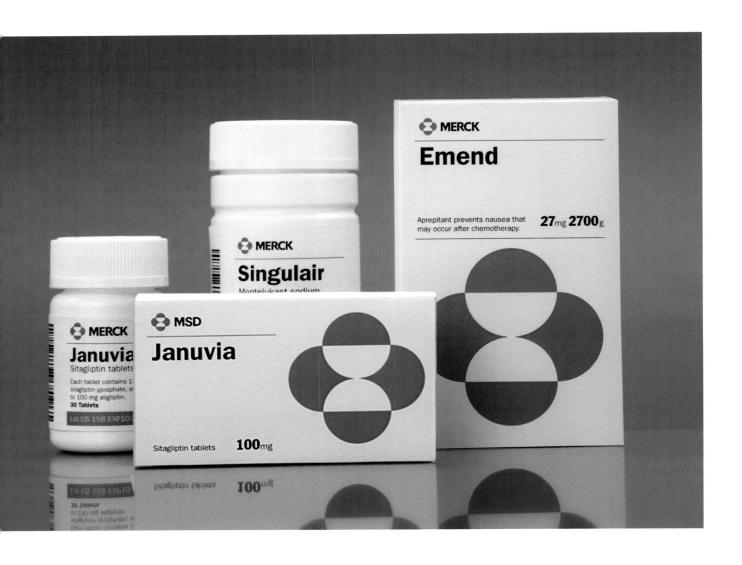

The Merck symbol and lettering style, combined with a consistent way of portraying division names, presents a unified company image (facing page).

On the packaging presentation samples shown above, the Merck and MSD products are clearly from the same source.

MERCK
Human Health

MERCK
Manufacturing Division

MERCK
Research Laboratories

MERCK
AgVet Division

MERCK
Vaccine Division

MERCK
Consumer Healthcare Group

MERCK
Specialty Chemicals Group

MSD

For many years **Burlington Industries** was the world's largest textile company. The bold symbol conveys the idea of weaving in a strong, clear way. The photo shows the entry lobby of the company's New York headquarters building.

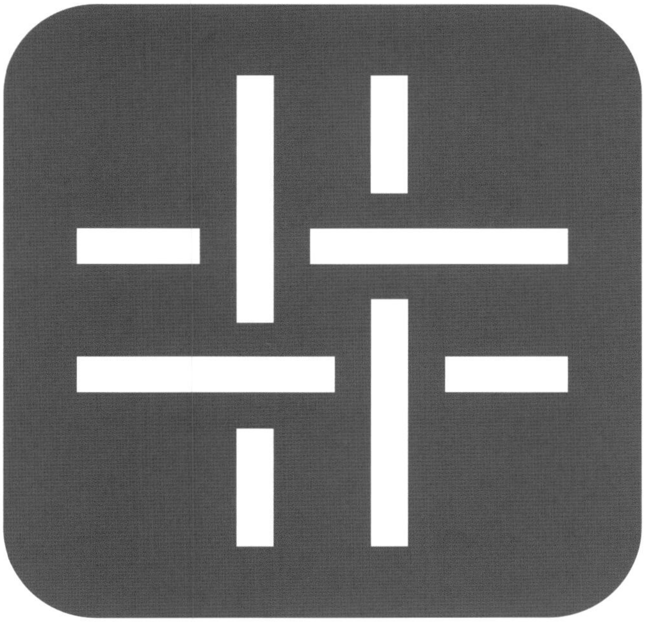

T I M E W A R N E R

When Time Inc. and Warner
Communications merged to
form **Time Warner**, a new
mark was needed to identify
this impressive new media
conglomerate. Steve Ross, then
the CEO, asked us to develop
a mark that could be used

throughout the organization.
Combining images of an eye and
an ear seemed a perfect way to
identify this company whose
products ranged from films
and magazines to music and
concerts.

Subsequent leadership decided
to emphasize the individual
components rather than the
overall corporation, and the
eye/ear symbol was designated
for Time Warner Cable, an
important corporate division.

The **Old Chatham Sheepherding Company** is a small dairy company that began with a single herd of 150 sheep in New York's Hudson Valley. As the company began to expand and ramp up production to almost 1,800 sheep, the company's owners realized they needed a memorable visual identity and in 1994 came to us to create it.

The Old Chatham Sheepherding Company is one of the smallest companies we've worked with, and yet the challenges we faced were as complex and demanding as for any of our largest corporate clients.

First, the name is long and doesn't particularly suggest cheese.

Next, as a very small company, Old Chatham had no advertising budget at all, so the company's labels, trucks, and packages had to be memorable and have enough visual impact to carry the brand's identity into the public mind.

Last, as with any client, we had to consider the real-world context of the product. In this case, the packaging would be viewed in the cold storage section of grocery stores, where consumers are usually uncomfortable and often overwhelmed with options. So the mark needed to be large enough to be seen and simple and friendly enough to be appealing.

If Chermayeff & Geismar is known for anything, it is for working almost exclusively within the modernist design tradition, which means simple, often abstract, spare, even minimalist shapes. But in the case of Old Chatham we determined that an illustrative mark or pictorial symbol would actually be more much effective and understandable because of the cluttered context in which it would always be viewed. Our solution was to create a one-of-a-kind mascot that would stand out in the grocery store and signal a one-of-a-kind, quality product.

The little sheep character is hand-drawn and so feels friendly and accessible. Its asymmetrically cocked ear provided attitude, personality—and recognizability. We took one more step toward the unusual by making the sheep black rather than white—not just because a white sheep wouldn't have as great a visual impact against the white of most grocery-store cheese displays, but also because the black sheep is more distinctive and unexpected. In all, the symbol connotes the product: artisanal and individual.

To make the Old Chatham packaging stand out on a cheese counter, the friendly black sheep symbol is generally seen standing on a field of green.

Scripps–Howard (now E. W. Scripps) is a major media company that has reinvented itself many times over recent years. But its roots, which go back to the 19th century, are in the newspaper business.

It was famous for publishing local papers throughout the country. In each, the Scripps ownership was symbolized by a rendering of a lighthouse. When Scripps decided to go public, we were asked to

develop a graphic identity for the company. An illustrative mark depicting a lighthouse seemed appropriate—given the idea of light as symbolizing the dissemination of knowledge— and had historical significance

to the company. This corporate brochure highlights some of the company's major assets, including some familiar cartoon characters.

the STJOE company annual report 1997

Language has everything to do with our practice. Often the name itself of a company provides an opportunity and an inspiration for a memorable visual.

In 1984, **Grey Advertising**—which at the time was the 10th largest ad agency in the United States—invited us to create a visual identity. We were intrigued by the challenges and possibilities inherent in the name. Most ad companies at the time were named after their founders, such as Benton & Bowles, Foote, Cone & Belding, or Doyle, Dane & Bernbach. The founders of Grey were two New York City natives named Valenstein and Fatt. Bucking the trend, they chose not to use their own names for their company.

Instead, they went with Grey, which was deliberately neutral, had four neat letters, and was referentially ambiguous. Still, it was essential that the identity have a clear and consistent impact, not only to attract potential clients, but also to recruit the best young graduates in the ad field.

Our design concept was simple: we took what "grey" brings to mind—a middle-ground value and unmemorable color—and turned it on its head.

Once we had made "grey" vermillion, there was no need for fancy lettering. The mark is bold and simple. It has a witty, provocative turn to it that is appropriate for the advertising world. The minor matter of making a ligature between the *E* and the *Y* made the wordmark slightly more distinctive—and easier to trademark in legal terms. With the distinctive ligature, the Grey wordmark is recognizable even in those rare instances such as newspaper ads when color is not available.

The initial presentation was to Ed Meyer, then chairman, and just a few other executives. They liked it and wanted it to be shown immediately to the larger group. They had one caveat: they asked that Chermayeff & Geismar be the ones to present the mark to the 75 account executives in the New York company. That way, if it backfired, it would be our responsibility. Fortunately, the design received a standing ovation. Because Grey was in the business, they got the joke right away.

As it turns out, Meyer has used the logo color twist as an icebreaker with every client since. The first slide in a presentation is always the Grey logo. "If the client asks why it's not gray," Meyer says, "then I know I'm in."

On the stationery system for
this global company, the GREY
is red, and the rest is gray.

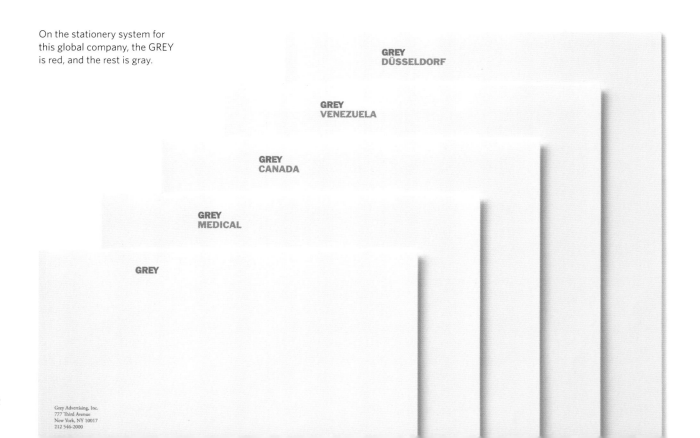

Grey Advertising, Inc.
777 Third Avenue
New York, NY 10017
212 546-2000

GREY

THE JEWISH CONVERSATION

The wordmark for Rabbi Yitzchok Itkin's outreach organization, **The Jewish Conversation**, provided us with another opportunity to create a visual pun. The intertwined letters suggest the dynamics of conversation.

A visualization of the idea of electricity for **The Electric Circus**, a popular disco in New York City, was achieved by mixing and overlapping positive and negative type, much in the spirit of the décor of the club.

THE ELECTRIC CIRCUS

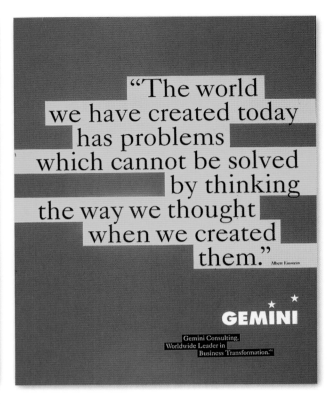

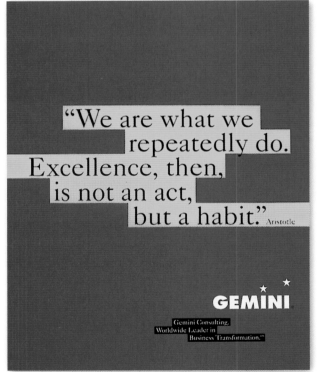

For **Gemini Consulting**, a major management consulting company, a simple play on the Gemini name seemed an appropriate starting point for a strong graphic identity. The twin Gemini stars give meaning and memorability to the name. Their position also suggests growth and progress.

A series of advertisements in *Fortune* magazine highlights provocative quotes in a style that was part of a larger program to establish Gemini as a thought leader.

GEMINI

The National Center on
Addiction and Substance
Abuse, founded by Joseph S.
Califano Jr., is housed at
Columbia University. To create
a memorable wordmark, the
letters are designed to form a
house, reflecting the acronym.

When Poets House first opened
in the East Village of New York
City, we introduced a very little
house, drawing on the suggestive
name—a symbol which appears
low-key and modest.

The most important directive we received from Warren Kuo—the Shanghai-based advertising director who, working as a consultant to the **Bank of Taipei**, reached out to us in 2008 to rebrand the bank—was that the bank wanted something Western, not Asian. "They want to be seen as international and global," he said—a perception, the bank hoped, would balance and complement its 90-year tradition as the familiar neighborhood bank.

Although this was the first project we completed without ever meeting the client personally, we worked very closely with Kuo and the bank executives via internet conference to fully understand their sensibilities, needs, and the demands of the local visual environment.

We got to work, exploring numerous concepts and design directions. We then pinned up all our sketches and identified the most successful and, importantly, "Western-looking" marks. Ultimately, we presented 11 marks over Skype to Warren. To our complete surprise, he saw Asian elements in all of them. To him, the bold, simple, geometric designs recalled chops, Chinese seals, and other Asian graphic motifs, while to us they seemed perfectly in keeping with international modernist design and our pursuit of simplicity and reduction.

We talked Kuo through the thinking process and rationale behind every mark, making the case for the international context of the simple, geometric designs. Together with Kuo, we carefully choreographed his presentation to the bank executives. They were thrilled.

The mark they ultimately adopted as the identifier for the bank grew out of the flag of the city of Taipei. A bold abstract symbol created from four blue circles also recalls the flower of the azalea tree, indigenous to the area. The square opening in the center of the form evokes security and protection.

At the end of the day, both client and designer came to terms with the extent to which the modernist movement and the abstract international style have learned from Asia.

The flag of the city of Taipei became the inspiration for the trademark's form and color.

The bold simplicity of this trademark allows it to be successfully used in a variety of materials and forms without losing its integrity.

Initial studies for the trademark are shown above.

大台北銀行

Jonathan Rose Companies is a diversified real estate policy, planning, and development company, with an emphasis on affordable green solutions. Created from a restrained palette of basic shapes—circles and squares—the mandala-like symbol designed to represent the company suggests the intricacy and interrelatedness of urban planning. The website design allows the viewer to delve into the rich variety of projects in an intuitive way.

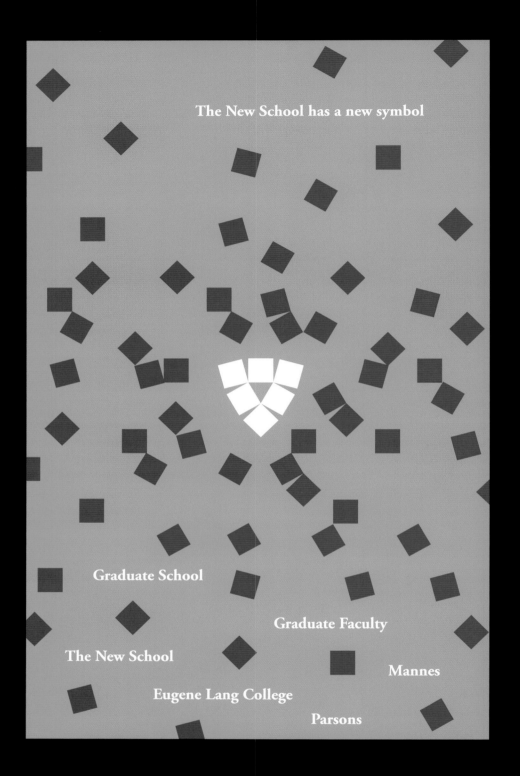

The New School has a new symbol

Graduate School

Graduate Faculty

The New School

Mannes

Eugene Lang College

Parsons

The New School consists of six major divisions, some with their own well-known names. A symbol was needed to tie together the divisions. So we designed a bold shield—the classic symbol for a university— out of six squares.

In the early 1960s, Boston's public transportation system was expanded in scope following the movement of people into the suburbs. Historically known as the MTA, the transit system was renamed the **Massachusetts Bay Transportation Authority** (MBTA) to reflect its new scale.

At that time, Ivan Chermayeff and Tom Geismar were two principals of Cambridge Seven Associates, a multidisciplinary firm of architects and designers in the Boston area. The young company was retained by the MBTA to develop an overall design program for the entire transit system, including stations, maps, signage, equipment markings, and so on, in an attempt to make the transportation experience more appealing to the public and its structure more legible.

Unlike our approach in most projects, in which we strive to create completely unique identities, in the case of the MBTA, our solution was so simple as to be generic—but by design. In shortening the MBTA to simply a *T*, the idea was to make the design an immediate symbol for a transportation system that would be recognizable in the cityscape at a distance, legible at any size, and useable in many different forms. We had been inspired in this effort by the red *T* symbol of Stockholm's municipal transit system because we thought that, of all public facilities, a transportation network should make sense at first glance to the stranger, regardless of his or her language. The result was perhaps the most straightforward symbol we've ever created.

The design of the *T* symbol was just the first part of an extensive graphics program, aimed at making the entire transit system more legible and comprehensible. In this case, our visual solution was also a linguistic one: the *T* can also be used in its own right as a word. One can "ride the T." Why *T*? Because there are so many transit-related words that begin with that letter: transportation, tram, trolley, train, track, and tunnel, to name a few.

More often than not, we mold our visuals to reflect or comment on the already existing language. But in this case, our design tried to affect the language itself. In Boston at least, it was successful. People very quickly picked up our shorthand reference for the transit system, and it is now an inseparable part of the colloquial language. We introduced people to the linguistic element of the design by opening our guidelines with a slogan that suggests the forward-looking spirit of the time: "Take the T and see..."

"Taking the T" has become part of the everyday parlance of the people of Boston and its surrounding communities.

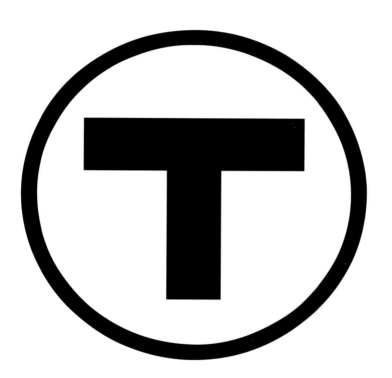

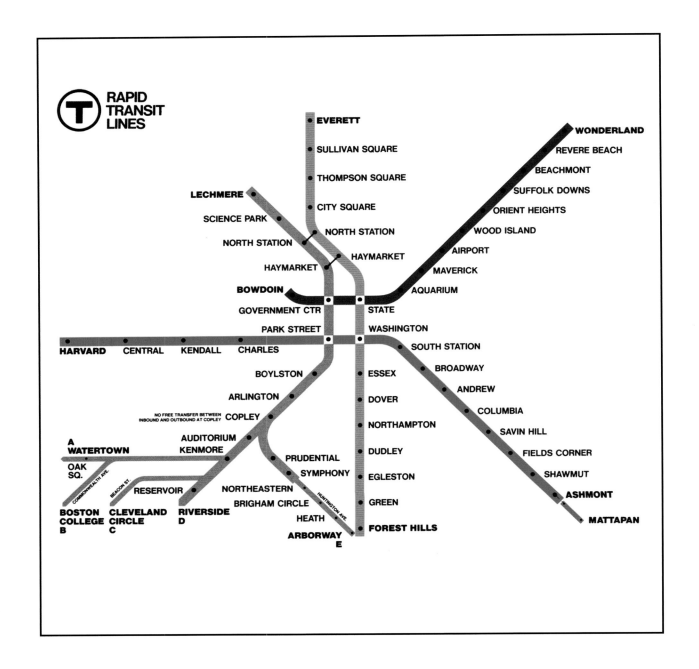

The original system map/diagram established color coding for the names of the lines. While the map has grown more complex over the years as the lines have expanded, the essential diagram still exists.

The photo on the facing page shows an early street sign marking an entrance to a T station.

19-21

Karsan is a diversified
automotive manufacturer in
Turkey that produces school
buses for the nation and
manufactures components for
major international car makers.
As in the previous case of the T,
the initial of the company was
our inspiration for the symbol.

Chermayeff & Geismar was
retained as the graphic design
team member in an international competition to design
the "Taxi of Tomorrow" for the
City of New York. Karsan was
among three finalists and was
the popular favorite.

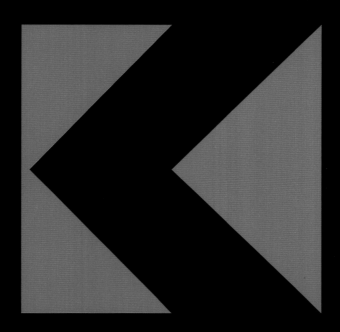

Focusing on the initial was our solution for **Princeton University Press**. The symbol (or colophon, in the language of publishing) is clearly based on the initial letter *P*, but you can also see in it a second letter *P* (for "press") and a sideways *U*. The bright orange is the university's color.

In the early 1990s, when the **National Geographic Society** found that it could no longer rely solely on magazine advertising and books to fund its extensive scientific, exploratory, and educational work, it decided to greatly expand its product lines and distribution channels. At that point, the National Geographic Society was becoming a much broader-based organization offering a wide range of publications, television programming, films, exhibitions, travel services, and a variety of other products and services to many audiences both in the U.S. and abroad.

By the late 1990s, this explosive growth had engendered a confusing array of brands and sub-brands, with dozens of variations in form and wording. With its offerings continuing to expand, National Geographic recognized that its inconsistent use was weakening the brand's identity, and that its existing design standards had become inadequate. Chermayeff & Geismar was then retained to develop a coherent, wide-ranging graphic identity program, one that would give National Geographic a more unified and consistent system of identification and also help convey the sense of quality and substance that has long distinguished the organization.

An extensive audit, combined with limited consumer research, showed that the simple yellow border logo inspired by the trademarked cover of National Geographic magazine is a strong brand identifier for National Geographic and that the color yellow itself generates relatively strong brand recognition. It was also clear that great photography is very much associated with National Geographic and that the two words "National Geographic" are, in the public's mind, used interchangeably for the brand and for the society.

Taking all this into account, we decided, for the basic signature, to retain the existing yellow-border mark, but to standardize its form and color and to combine it with the name "National Geographic" set in a bold new, proprietary lettering style.

A clear size relationship between the two basic elements was fixed in order to establish a strong, highly recognizable graphic identity. In doing so, we also eliminated all the function and division names (except "Channel") that had previously been directly tied into the National Geographic name and instead developed a system for incorporating division names and titles separately from the basic signature and limiting their use.

Beyond the basic signature and guidelines for usage, recommendations were made for the extensive use of the color yellow, especially for product packaging; the use wherever possible of appropriate and striking photography; a standard way to incorporate a message about the society and its purpose; and how, without restrictions on layout and design, the use of strong, clean contemporary design can help update perceptions of National Geographic.

Since agencies, filmmakers, and others who use the National Geographic identity are located throughout the world, an extensive online set of guidelines was developed. These guidelines not only explain the basic rules and philosophy of the identity system, but also allow authorized users to download approved trademark variations, alphabets, and photography.

With National Geographic, our attitude was not to reinvent the wheel, but rather to retain and emphasize those attributes that the public clearly associates with the society, and to establish a simple, coherent identity system that works across a wide spectrum of product lines. The rollout of National Geographic's new identity was so seamless as to be practically unnoticeable, but the house was now in order.

NATIONAL GEOGRAPHIC

The National Geographic "housemark" (symbol and name) is used to identify a broad range of material in a variety of media. As shown on the book covers on the facing page, we recommended that the logo be used on a dark background whenever feasible to give maximum impact to the yellow box symbol.

The National Geographic Channel is the one exception where the name can be expanded to include another word. In broadcast, the yellow box symbol alone often appears in the lower right of the screen to clearly identify the channel.

NATIONAL GEOGRAPHIC

NATURE LIBRARY

BIRDS

SHARKS

FROGS

FROGS

New York University is a truly urban school, with offices, departments, and classes spread considerably beyond its lower Manhattan campus. The university spaces are sometimes tucked into buildings that house a business or retail store as its most visible occupant.

Without a clear visual identity, it was almost as though the university melted into the city landscape. In 1972, New York University asked us to develop a strong graphic identity that would help hold together its geographically sprawling campus.

In order to design an appropriate identity for the university, we looked to its past for imagery. NYU's traditional seal contained an intricate scene of runners moving forward, following the beacon of a lit torch. To create a simpler and more visible icon, we eliminated the background images and the runners and focused instead on the idea of torch and flame—a traditional symbol of knowledge.

The simplified torch shines in white as a flame in the darkness of purple, with the school initials placed below the torch when needed. The purple color, too, has had a long history with the university. NYU's sports teams have always been known as the "Violet." It's a distinctive, vivid color that calls attention to itself when used on a flag hung from a city building or painted on the side of a university shuttle bus.

NYU's urban campus continues to grow at an extraordinary rate; in 2010, there were more than 50,000 students. The torch symbol and the purple color have continued to flag the university's spaces, much like geo-tags that indicate points of interest on an interactive map. As a result, NYU is now perceived to exist almost as a singular, enormous campus, wherever the identity is visible.

The purple torch banners can be seen all over Lower Manhattan, where NYU occupies dozens of buildings. Left: previous trademark.

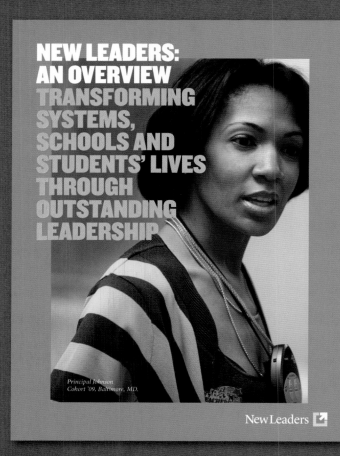

NEW LEADERS: AN OVERVIEW
TRANSFORMING SYSTEMS, SCHOOLS AND STUDENTS' LIVES THROUGH OUTSTANDING LEADERSHIP

Principal Johnson
Cohort '09, Baltimore, MD.

New Leaders

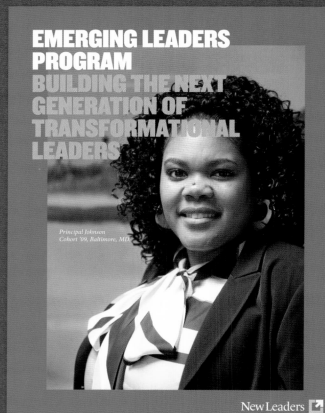

EMERGING LEADERS PROGRAM
BUILDING THE NEXT GENERATION OF TRANSFORMATIONAL LEADERS

Principal Johnson
Cohort '09, Baltimore, MD.

New Leaders

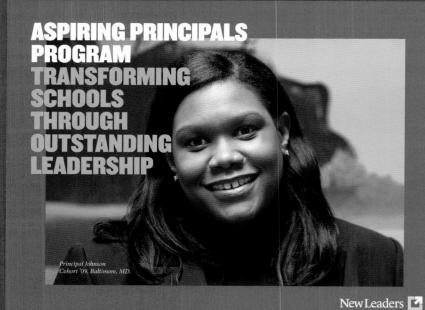

ASPIRING PRINCIPALS PROGRAM
TRANSFORMING SCHOOLS THROUGH OUTSTANDING LEADERSHIP

Principal Johnson
Cohort '09, Baltimore, MD.

New Leaders

The symbol we designed for **New Leaders**, the primary organization in the United States for school-principal training, illustrates the dynamics of leadership, which is at the heart of organization's mission.

The visual language features photo portraits and biographies of successful New Leaders principals in colorful, bold frames that echo the symbol and add distinction.

India has emerged as one of the fastest growing economies in the world, but reaching its full potential requires great improvement to its infrastructure facilities, which at present are not sufficient to meet the growing demands of its economy. As a result, the Indian government has put a high priority on the extensive development of the country's infrastructure. To do so, the government has been actively engaged in involving the private sector to meet the growing demand for roads, electric power, airports, inland waterways, public transport, and other improvements.

SEW Infrastructure is a privately held company founded in the 1950s as Southern Engineering Works. In recent years, it has grown from a regional to a national player, with major projects throughout the nation. To get away from the regional connotation of the legal name—and as a shorthand version of it—the company began using its seal/monogram with the initials SEW as its primary logo. But the seal was not very distinguished or contemporary looking, and the leadership recognized the need for a more modern, striking (and legible) identity that could facilitate the company's growing stature.

The challenge was to find a way to present the abbreviated name the company desired, SEW, in a bold and appropriate way. But the initials themselves also presented a challenge, as they form the common word *sew*, a word completely irrelevant to the company's activities.

During a five-day trip to India, we visited a few of the infrastructure projects SEW had under construction, from a metro system for Mumbai and a highway near Hyderabad to a monumental dam and power station two hours outside the city of Indore. More than 4,000 people were working on that last project alone.

These epic structures inspired our design solution. We reversed the *S, E,* and *W* out of three broad, vertical bars to connote the massive columns or pillars common to many of the company's projects. In addition to being bold, legible, and expressive, this design addresses an additional parameter: pronunciation. The three letters are clearly separated by lines to guide the reader to pronounce them not as an acronym but as three initials. The letters were rendered as italic forms, and each is partially obscured on the left, as if in motion through structures—an expression of the company's core mission to build infrastructure that facilitates the movement of water, vehicles, and people.

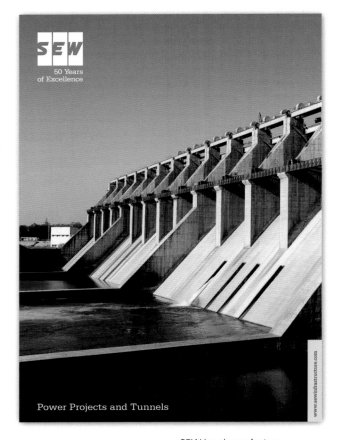

SEW brochures feature the trademark against striking photographs of the giant projects that inspired it.

Previous trademark

SEW

The Museum of Contemporary Art
Los Angeles

The Museum of Contempora
Los Angeles

A Prospectus

A
Corporate
Luncheon

An
Afternoon
at the
Office

The

Expressing an instituion's mission using the design of the letters became a playful exercise for the **Museum of Contemporary Art, Los Angeles**. We noticed that three of the letters in the initials are essentially a square, a circle, and a triangle—the most basic geometric shapes. With the addition of the classic lowercase C, the resulting trademark identifies the museum. The basic geometric components of the logo are also used in artistic and humorous ways for invitations, programs, tickets, and other printed materials.

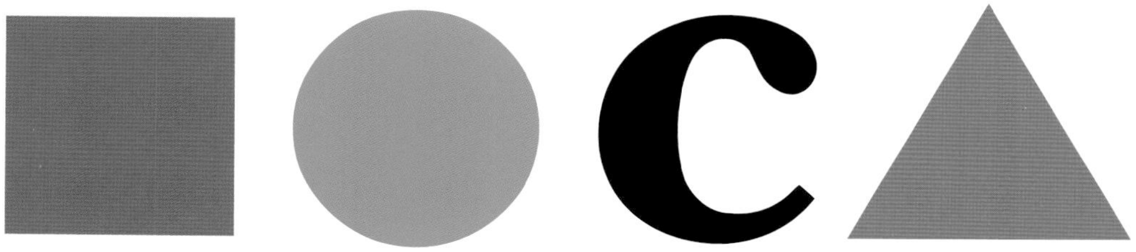
C

Every decade between 1909 and 1970, Congress called a giant gathering of experts and organizations to the White House to discuss issues pertaining to the nation's children. The 1970 **White House Conference on Children** was the largest. (It would also wind up being the last to be held.)

The bipartisan congressional committee directing the conference approached us to create a single graphic identity to unify the various publications, posters, invitations, and letterheads produced by this giant initiative. Our design would need to give a dose of humanity to the conference publications.

We came up with a simple idea: two flowers—a larger one and a smaller one—suggesting a parent and child, but also suggesting growth, development, and vitality.

Conceptualizing the mark was one thing, but rendering it was another. A simple idea can sometimes require a tremendous amount of time, effort, and technique to execute.

To begin with, we felt that the mark should reinforce the notion of childhood. We thought that the rendition of the symbol should look free and hand-drawn, which would make it seem less commercial and more personal and expressive. To push the concept further, we thought that it should look as though a child had drawn it.

But how do you make a mark look as though a child created it? The obvious answer is to go find a child to draw it. So we asked a few children to do the "childlike" drawing.

It was a complete disaster: The actual child-produced drawings were charming but did not look childlike at all. The children were trying so hard to draw something "good" that the results lacked the intuitive gesture we were looking for.

We needed an adult's version of a childlike drawing. But how do you achieve that? Another technique we tried was drawing and walking at the same time. We produced dozens of pages of drawings, but ultimately, success came with another old trick: switching to the less dominant hand, which is sure to produce a slightly imperfect and clumsy result.

And it worked. Drawn with the nondominant hand, it had the right level of precision but also a loose, gestural quality. The final drawing is a focused image, rendered in bold, immediate brushstrokes. It is so simple as to come close to abstraction, which is a significant departure for political graphic design. It was a versatile enough concept that we were able to create a series of variations upon it to go along with the different themes and focuses of the conference.

The silver lining to the discontinuation of the White House Conference on Children has been that, as the last exemplars in this series of important public inquiries, the 1970 publications with the two-flowers mark have become invaluable reference materials, and with them, the identity also lives on.

The drawing of a parent and child, inspired by children's art, also suggests growth and accomplishment.

On the next spread: reports resulting from the White House Conference on Children concerned issues such as education, upbringing, health, and a child's place in society. The art for the covers used the humanized flowers to suggest the specific content of each report.

Myths of
Education

Expressions
of Identity

Child
Care

Future of
Learning

Changing
Families

Rights of
Children

Keeping
Children
Healthy

Injured

Making
Children
Healthy

Children
Without
Prejudice

Environment

Child
Development
and
Mass Media

Crisis in
Values

Creativity and
the Learning
Process

Communicating
the Law

Family
Planning
Family
Economics

Leisure
Time

Child
Service
Institutions

Young Audiences—Arts for Learning is a nonprofit organization that works with schools, the arts community, and private and public sectors to provide arts education to children. A childlike drawing of a sun seemed an appropriate and lively mark for this organization, and it has become a well-established icon within the education community.

When Mobil agreed to sponsor the Young Audiences program in the Washington, D.C., area, we thanked the company by having its red *O* come up over the horizon on this press kit (top left).

The folder (bottom left) shows the photography and typographic style used for Young Audiences—Arts for Learning materials over many years.

New York's very own circus in a magical all new show with the Nanjing Acrobatic Troupe under the Trump Tent at Lincoln Center Oct. 27–Jan. 2

The **Big Apple Circus** is a small, one-ring circus in the traditional European style. It's important that their graphic identity conveys a warm, friendly feeling, which was achieved both with the choice of subject matter and with its hand-cut forms. Since the show changes each year, the graphics also vary, but they retain a consistent visual language. A juggling baby elephant in this poster (left) actually inspired the circus to buy a baby elephant. The next year's poster (above) led to the puchase of a baby buffalo.

The symbol on the facing page turns the Big Apple into a circus apple with its stars taken from the decorative motif on the inside of the circus tent.

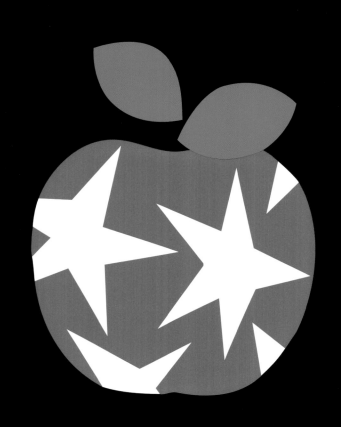

In the early 1990s, we were asked to create a new visual identity for the Spanish-language television giant **Univision**. The previous trademark for the network greatly resembled the mark for Televisa, the largest television network in Mexico and formerly Univision's parent company. By breaking the visual identification with the Mexican network, Univision was looking to position itself as the leading American network for Spanish speakers.

As we performed our initial audit to determine the client's vision of itself and its future, we asked Univision's executives whether they wanted a visual mark to reflect, in some way, the Latino heritage of its audience. Their directive, instead, was to make the Univision branding appear more multinational. As one of its directors put it, they wanted a mark that was "more IBM than salsa."

The wish to be seen as international, and not specifically Latino, freed us from having to make particular, concrete, cultural references and allowed us to try to develop a bold symbol that was appropriate, especially for television.

The mark is derived from the initial letter *U* in the company name and is broken up into four colorful panes. The top left pane, which is identical to the lower forms

but flipped on its side, gives the mark its unique character. While overall the form is clearly a *U*, the flipped pane also makes it into a colorful abstract bird or flower. The bright color scheme, while clearly appropriate to Latino culture, is universal in its appeal.

While Univision has had a series of owners over the years, the symbol and name have remained constants. The company has undertaken initiatives in many related fields, and today Univision Communications Inc. is the premier Spanish-language media company in the United States.

The Univision symbol combines the notion of a capital letter *U* and a colorful bird.

Right: early design sketches.
Below: previous trademark.

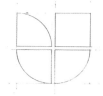

Beehouse is a fashion and lifestyle brand geared to young people in Seoul, Korea. The bold symbol takes the hexagonal shape integral to a beehive's structure and combines it with a vertical stem to clearly form a distinctive initial letter *B*. Shown above is a typical Beehouse magazine advertisement.

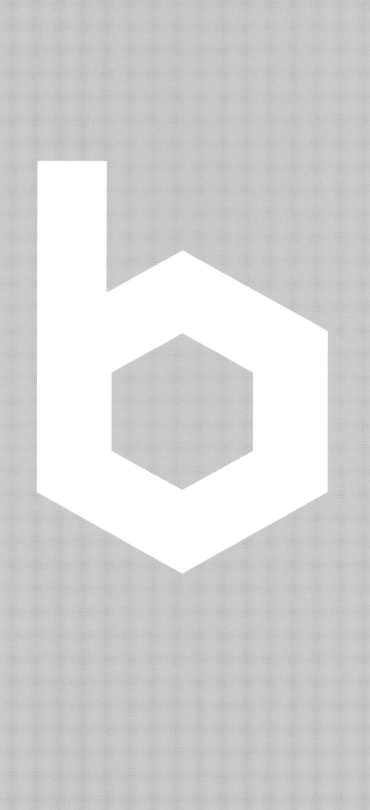

Giving a bank a symbol is an effective way to make it visible, especially if the institution has a long name. We had certainly proved as much in the 1960s with the Chase Manhattan Bank trademark. Since then, symbols representing banks have become ubiquitous. So when in 1981 the **Dime Savings Bank of New York** came to us for an identity, we had to seriously consider developing a symbol.

However, we recognized that the bank was universally referred to simply as "Dime," so the first thing we did was shorten the name. Once we had an appropriate, four-letter name like Dime, a well-considered wordmark was all we needed to make an immediate impression. This was especially true once the letters were made red.

To add a distinctive, pictorial element to the mark, we wanted to make a reference to the very thing "dime" means, i.e., the small thin coin. The challenge here was that, in all capital letters, a dot on the *I* in dime still goes unnoticed. Once we added an unnecessary dot as a period at the end of the word, however, the dot over the capital *I* took on visual meaning, and the trademark for the Dime Savings Bank of New York came to life, as both name and image.

The ultradeep dimensional letters of the branch signs enhance the boldness of this distinctive trademark.

DIME.

Harvard Maintenance provides cleaning and security services for major corporate, educational, and industrial facilities across the nation. To make the name memorable and to distinguish it from the famous university, we extended the middle letter *V* into a check mark, emphasizing reliability, efficiency, and expertise. In the context of the identity system as a whole, the wordmarks of the various services offered look like a successful checklist.

HARVARD® MAINTENANCE

HIRSHHORN

SPRING/SUMMER 2010

HIRSHHORN

FALL 2010

HIRSHHORN

SUMMER 2011

HIRSHHORN

SPRING 2011

The **Hirshhorn Museum and Sculpture Garden** is the Smithsonian's contemporary art museum on the Mall in Washington, D.C. In order to attract more visitors, tourists, and locals, the museum needed a stronger visual presence. Playing with the rare appearance of three *H*s in the name, we developed a bold wordmark. The letter *H* on its own is used in varying sizes and colors to form eye-catching graphic images used for posters, flyers, the cover of the museum's quarterly magazine, signage, and more.

HIRSHHORN

Rahmi M. Koç, the chairman of **Koç Holding**, is a collector of art and antiquities, a discerning and sensitive observer of the many creative worlds that cross his path. In the early 1970s, the Koç family firm—which owned part or all of more than 110 separate companies—represented Mobil Oil in Turkey. Rahmi Koç admired the design of the Mobil wordmark and inquired who had designed it. He came to New York to meet us and discuss the possibility of Chermayeff & Geismar's developing an identity for his family's firm.

And so, in the early 1970s, we took on the task of designing a symbol for Koç.

Holding companies are businesses that operate mostly out of the public eye. They don't often have striking visual identities, and even today it is uncommon for them to have pictorial marks. Rahmi Koç already knew when he came to us that he wanted to be more visible than the average holding company.

We developed a pictorial, even pictographic solution. "Koç" means "ram" in Turkish. And the simplified red ram's horns now identifies companies owned in whole or in part by this powerful Turkish family.

Since then, our relationship with Rahmi Koç and Koç Holding has grown to be our longest-standing relationship with a client. Chermayeff & Geismar has designed graphic identities for a number of the major manufacturers and companies owned by the Koç Holding Company: from fuel companies, heavy-vehicle factories, and commercial banks to retail appliance, home-improvement, and tourism companies. We also became involved with the graphic identity program for the Rahmi M. Koç Industrial Museum, a vast collection of artifacts ranging from superbly restored automobiles to a WWII German submarine brought up from the depths of the Baltic Sea.

Our approach to design and process for the development of each and every one of these identities were no different than for any of our other clients. But one aspect of the branding task that is often the most challenging—convincing the client of the merit of our favored solution—was effortless in the case of Koç companies. Rahmi Koç, who as the head of the holding company had the last word, was always perfectly opinionated and reasonable, but also treated us like doctors. And so, time and time again, our recommendations were adopted without challenge.

The symbol is widely used for the numerous business entities and enterprises owned in part or in whole by the Koç family.

Owned by Koç Holding, **Arçelik** is is the major Turkish manufacturer of refrigerators, stoves, and other kitchen appliances in Turkey. The wordmark is set within a dynamic red shape suggestive of rolled steel, which is the meaning of the company's name in Turkish.

Another Koç-controlled company, **Aygaz** is the major liquid petroleum gas supplier in Turkey, with service locations around the country. The logo is a bold wordmark that emphasizes the angled strokes of the letters and is simple enough to be stenciled on gas containers.

AYGAZ

Tüpraş is an integrated petroleum company and Turkey's largest industrial enterprise. The name stands for Turkish Petroleum Refineries Company. The Tüpraş symbol suggests a drop of oil, but also forward and upward motion. The Tüpraş name is set in the same bold lettering style used for many Koç Holding businesses to help tie them together in advertising and promotion.

Opet was a small, family-owned oil company acquired by Koç Holding. A bold new identity and color scheme were designed, with emphasis on the Opet wordmark. Based on this wordmark, a full alphabet was developed for use on product names, advertising headlines, fuel grade designations, and elsewhere. A full line of packaging was also designed for sales at Opet stations as well as retail outlets throughout the country.

opet

The trademark for the **Rahmi M. Koç Industrial Museum** (above) and **Koç University** (right) are variations on the ram's horn identity established for Koç Holding.

In 1987, Rupert Murdoch's News Corporation acquired Harper & Row, a New York publishing firm that had roots in the early 19th century. Three years later, News Corporation acquired William Collins, a famous U.K. publisher founded in the 1820s, with plans to consolidate the two publishing houses.

In 1990, Chermayeff & Geismar was asked to design an identity for the new combined company, **HarperCollins Publishers**.

Harper & Row's symbol depicted hands passing a torch—a classical allusion to the dissemination of knowledge—and had been updated and redesigned since its first introduction in 1845.

William Collins was represented by a symbol of a fountain, another classical Greek allusion to the idea of wisdom as a fount or spring. It was drawn with a substantial plinth, a wide dish, and multiple jets of water forming a tall semicircle—a distinctive, yet complex image.

An important part of the job, as was relayed to us, was to retain as much as possible of both the Harper and the Collins identities, each of which had built enormous reputational equity over the centuries. To make matters even more complicated, Harper & Row and William Collins each had separate imprints that published everything from theological texts to children's primers, so the overall identity system of the new company would need to tie together all the names of these different monikers.

There was no question in our minds that a single symbol for the company was needed, rather than a long wordmark that would inevitably have to be reduced to fit into small spaces. A pictorial mark would also make the necessary visual impact in the place a publishing company's identity is most visible—on the spines of books—and would easily work as a unifying symbol for all of the different imprints.

However, the existing symbols of the two companies were much too detailed and complex for us to simply combine them. Instead, we turned to one of the most essential principles of modernism: reduction—not only in form but also in concept.

So in place of the references of torch and fountain, we extracted the essential element of each symbol: the fountain became water and the torch simply fire. The reduction paradoxically yields a broader, more applicable idea. Instead of specific allusions—this fountain, in this tradition, translates to that myth—we now featured basic and universal elements.

The second step was formal reduction: rendering the two elements as simple forms with a graphic commonality. The resulting combined symbol, composed of two separate shapes, presents a visual partnership of two equal—yet distinct—entities.

To complement the new symbol, we came up with a straightforward typographic solution for rendering the merged company's name. We set off the bold, modernist simplicity of the symbol with a classic typeface, thus evoking a sense of the companies' long tradition. We removed the space between the two words—thus emphasizing the new company's unity—while retaining the capital letters for the two names, to remind the public that these had previously been separate companies.

Previous Harper & Row trademark

Previous William Collins trademark

Torch and fountain were joined when the two publishing giants William Collins and Harper & Row joined forces. The symbol for the new entity took the basic elements of each of the companies' symbols, fire and water, and combined them into a single trademark.

Most identity designers—ourselves included—present multiple design alternatives to a client. This is because most design options have pluses and minuses. For example, a mark may be light and elegant but have less visual impact; another may be perfectly suited to the client conceptually but be more formally complex, and so on. However, in rare cases, we recognize pure serendipity. The HarperCollins water and fire icon was one such case. We therefore diverged from usual practice and presented just the one concept to the client.

In the wake of the technological revolution that changed the publishing industry and caused more and more readers to buy electronic texts rather than physical books, an unexpected strength of our HarperCollins colophon emerged. The simplicity of the design has thrived in the digital realm, which demands legibility in smaller sizes than even on a book's spine.

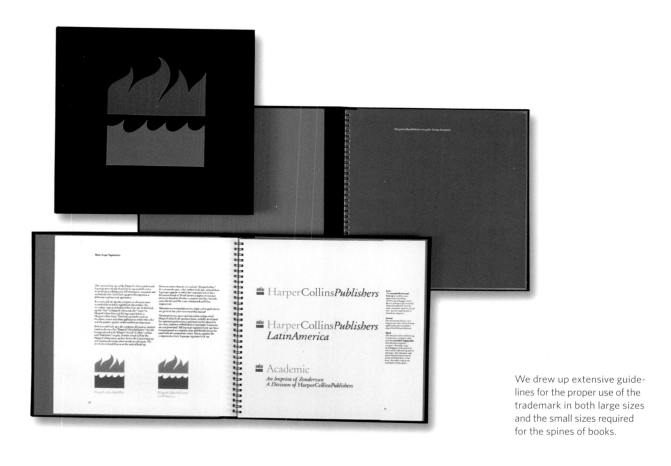

We drew up extensive guidelines for the proper use of the trademark in both large sizes and the small sizes required for the spines of books.

M.D.

Harper
Collins

Collins

EDITED BY LYNNE ATTWOOD

Pandora

AS
h TAMARKIN

Harper
Business

The Dubai-based Mesforoosh family had been metal and steel traders around the Middle East for three generations when the youngest son, Amir, contacted us in 2008 regarding a corporate identity dilemma.

The family's company, **Amesco**, had been using a mark that everyone loved. It was a bold, simple, and most important, appropriate design, composed of three interlocking abstract *A* shapes. All three members of the Mesforoosh family involved with Amesco have names that start with the letter *A*, so the mark was truly tailored for them.

But there was a major problem. Although the mark was interesting and meaningful to the family members, it was not original. In fact, it was quite a common design, and they would not be able to own and register it as the company's trademark. As the company was expanding its reach to Russia, Asia, and beyond, it needed an original mark.

This assignment turned out to be quite challenging. The parameters were clear and strict: to design a symbol that evoked three As. However, throughout the process, we were haunted by the previous mark. Unusable as it was, it was an iconic image and set an extremely high bar. As we worked to create a new, original form, we were determined to present only those designs that were as exciting or even more so.

After two complete rounds of concept explorations, we arrived at a successful solution: three bars, suggesting steel beams, that meet within a circle to create three revolving As. Amir and his father and brother all loved the mark, which has now been legally trademarked internationally as Amesco's own.

We designed a simple, modern website to represent the company's offerings, using a reserved color palette of blues and grays to add continuity for Amesco's identity.

The previous trademark (below) was too common a design to be proprietary.

Symbols can derive from letterforms while being expressive.

Starting with a letter *P* and
growing into concentric circles,
this trademark identifies
Parkhouse, a real estate arm of
the Mitsubishi conglomerate
in Japan.

Screen Gems is a major entertainment company, producing
movies and television shows.
The symbol suggests a reel of
film that forms an active capital
S and *G* for Screen Gems.

In 1976, the United States of America celebrated its 200th birthday with parties, events, and presentations all across the nation. The U.S. Treasury struck an edition of special bicentennial commemorative coins, states issued special bicentennial license plates, and of course government officials from the president down to the local mayor participated in celebrations of every sort. In order to present a visually coordinated face to the nation on its birthday, the bipartisan Bicentennial Commission contacted Chermayeff & Geismar to produce an official emblem for the **American Revolution Bicentennial**. The design challenge was to find a way to represent the U.S. without directly employing the classic (and overused) symbols of the nation: the flag, the eagle, etc.

The design of this symbol suggests the bunting with which parades and grandstands are festooned during patriotic events. While this mark includes all of the elements of the American flag—the stars, the stripes, and the colors—it uses them in a new way.

When we made our formal presentation to the Bicentennial Commission, its members liked the design, but were concerned that, unadorned, it might not be sufficiently governmental. They wanted a trademark that would look official and be easy to protect under trademark law. An emblematic symbol, the mark wouldn't be available for just anyone to use—even a state or local government that wanted to place it on a book or a souvenir, for example, had to apply for a license from the Bicentennial Commission. To address this request for a more authoritative look, we added a ring of type around the star. With this addition, the mark was officially adopted.

The symbol was put into use all over the country. We developed extensive guidelines for how the mark was to be used and formats for special wording for various states, cities, and towns. The mark helped unite the diverse events and celebrations, reports, and studies that were undertaken throughout the country.

The bicentennial mark has appeared on thousands of applications, from a tiny postage stamp to the side of a giant shuttle silo. It was even placed by NASA on the planet Mars. This wide size range is perhaps the most extreme example of the important test we give all our trademark designs: every one must be compelling and interesting enough to be rendered in a large format, yet simple and focused enough to work on a very small scale.

The symbol for the United States Bicentennial celebration grows out of the bunting commonly used at political rallies, but does so in a dynamic and meaningful way. Extensive guidelines for the use of the trademark were published as a brochure.

PHOTO COURTESY OF NASA

The bicentennial symbol was widely used during the celebration year, even appearing in a postage stamp. The mark even made it all the way to Mars, as seen here on NASA's *Viking 1* lander in 1977.

U.S. POSTAGE 8¢

AMERICAN REVOLUTION BICENTENNIAL 1776-1976

50 Years   The Museum of Modern Art

Another approach for designing an anniversary mark is to put the focus on the number of years being celebrated.

On the occasion of **The Museum of Modern Art's 50th Anniversary**, a bold mark was designed using an artistic play on the numerals 5 and 0. The design was used extensively on print materials, banners, and signs. The shopping bag shown above featured an animated version of the trademark, with the elements coming together to form the symbol.

Armani Exchange's 20th Anniversary was commemorated with the A|XX mark shown on the facing page. Having grown naturally from the core Armani Exchange trademark, the anniversary trademark was able to be used in place of the standard identity for the entire year's advertising.

TWENTY YEARS

The **Milwaukee Institute of Art and Design** is a long name that does not roll easily off the tongue. So everyone calls the school "My-Ad." The acronym MIAD, however, does not quite read the way it is pronounced.

In 2006, the then new MIAD president came to us to create a new identity for the school. The existing trademark was a rather old-fashioned-looking seal: busy and not very legible. It also did not convey a sense of either tradition or stature the way better-known university seals do.

When we began the work, we saw an opportunity to do more than simply modernize or update the existing identity. And the pronunciation of this unusual shorthand was on our mind.

It is always preferable to design the visual to reflect the colloquial reality on the ground rather than to try to change what people already say. With that in mind we drew the four letters in very bold sans-serif characters and divided them according to the two syllables, stacking them on top of one another so that it actually reads phonetically as "My-Ad."

This simple intervention, along with a distinctive color scheme, made the acronym visually memorable. But more important, it ensured that the pronunciation would be correct every time.

The shortened MIAD, pronounced "My-Ad," is what everyone calls this school, so the logo focuses on that acronym. The sketch of stacked letters at far left suggests an idea for a sculpture to mark the front entrance to the school. Near left: previous trademark.

MI
AD

The symbol for **Pilobolus Dance Theatre**, a modern dance company, was first introduced on a poster announcing the group's initial run of performances at the Joyce Theater. The name is broken onto three lines and stacked, in an arrangement that suggests the many stacked and odd formations that the Pilobolus dancers assume in their performances.

PI L
O O
BO
LUS

PIL
OBO
LUS

Shinsegae, a major, long-established Korean department store chain, contacted us in 1999 to design a corporate trademark that could also be used as a motif to beautify its shopping bags, wrapping papers, general packaging, and its stores.

Because the company had also recently diversified into other areas such as real estate and construction, the directors wanted an emblem that would emphasize its traditional reputation as a luxury retailer. As a department store, Shinsegae's customer base is mostly women, and we were asked to take that fact into consideration.

The decorative has long been considered the enemy of the modern, but there's an exception to every adage. Even a die-hard modernist must recognize those exceptional situations that call for decorative design.

Given Shinsegae's corporate profile and stated goals, we decided that a decorative, floral mark was exactly what was needed.

To forge the proposed design, each petal for this flower was cut individually with scissors. The resulting flower mark looks handmade—it's not perfect or symmetrical, which gives it a natural feel.

For a floral mark, the Shinsegae symbol remains simple and, quite literally, pared-down. It is also impressive when illuminated on the side of the Shinsegae store in Busan, Korea, that was unveiled in 2009 and officially recognized by Guinness as the largest department store in the world.

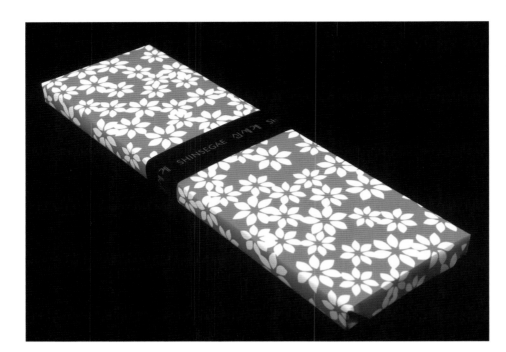

(Previous page) For Shinsegae, we designed wordmarks in both Korean and English to go with the symbol. As we had done for other Korean clients, we created two-sided business cards with Korean and English on opposite sides.

The flower symbol, a decorative device in the first place, lent itself to even more decorative uses in packaging, wrapping papers, and shopping bags in a country where the giving of beautifully wrapped gifts is an especially important cultural practice.

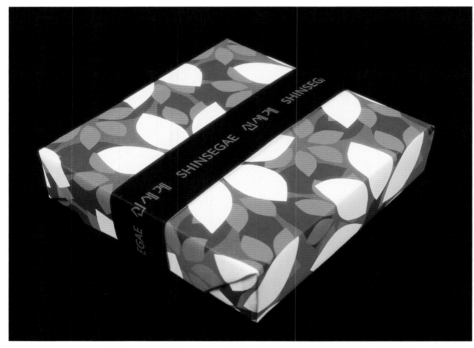

SHINSEGAE

SHINSEGAE

신세계

본 점 : 02) 310-1234
영동포점 : 02)939-1234
미 아 점 : 02) 344-1234
인 천 점 : 032)430-1234
광 주 점 : 06)360-1234

In the late 1950s, the Haloid Company developed the first practical copying machine, using a process dubbed xerography. Looking to identify its brand with its process, the company changed its name to Haloid Xerox. In 1961, in recognition of the commercial potential of its new products, the name was again changed, this time to **Xerox Corporation**. A new logo was developed that featured the word Xerox in thick and thin stroked letters which emphasized the diagonal thrust of the two X's and the R by giving them "tails" and placing the name above the word "Corporation."

Within a few years Xerox became one of the fastest growing businesses in the U.S. The new in-house design director, Jack Hough, asked Chermayeff & Geismar to establish an overall design attitude reflective of this dynamic, technologically advanced company.

While designing a wide variety of materials, we found the logo to be cumbersome and fussy and over a period of a couple years cut off the "tails," removed "Corporation," and made the lettering simpler and bolder. All this was done to make a cleaner, more confident and protectable mark, and it was done in a way that didn't sacrifice any of the equity that had been so rapidly established in that unique name. The result is a kind of classic mark that achieves distinction and memorability by relying more on the unusual name and the unusual combination of letters (an X at either end) than on elaborate graphics.

The company continued to expand substantially throughout the 1960s and early 1970s. In some ways it was the Apple of its time, and many now-common computing technologies—such as the first true personal computer, the mouse, and the graphical user interface that formed the basis of the Macintosh system—were first developed in Xerox's Palo Alto Research Center (PARC). During this time, Xerox was so far ahead of the technology curve that many of PARC's best ideas ended up being developed and exploited by others, among them the then young Steve Jobs.

The goal of the design program was to convey a sense of excellence and clarity in all visual expressions, from letterheads to advertisements, from product identification to plant signs. To help achieve uniformity and clarity of identification, we developed an extensive set of detailed graphic standards for items commonly used throughout this increasingly international company. At the same time, to further convey the innovative spirit of the company, we undertook a wide variety of specific design projects, such as annual reports, brochures, and package designs. To each of these we brought a sense of creativity and liveliness, as these kinds of materials needed to be continually fresh and new to reflect the essence of a rapidly evolving company that helped to define the new business of communications.

Previous trademark

XEROX

An industrial organization demands results and Xerox can be no exception. Yet, Xerox also must search for new ideas on which to create its future. For the professional scientist or engineer these demands of new ideas and subsequently acceptable results may cause a personal dilemma. Quite often, as the professional achieves results, he is rewarded with managerial advancement. As he becomes involved in matters of administration he must necessarily move further and further away from the technical specialty for which he was originally trained.

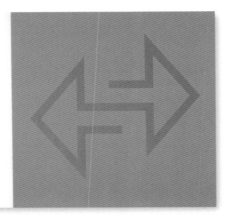

This alternate avenue is the "dual ladder" of advancement for professional scientists and engineers at Xerox. It opens a new method of personal reward for the individual contributor —that person whose research talents and/or achievements are recognized to be of the highest order.

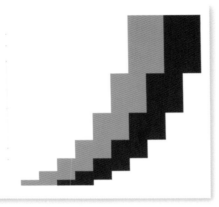

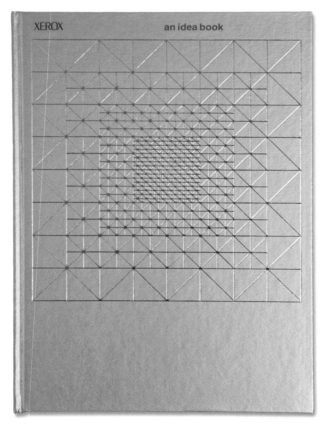

To reinforce Xerox's position as a leading technology company, many distinctive publications were developed. The example at top is from a brochure showing engineers how they could advance in the company without having to assume extensive managerial tasks. The brochure at left uses imaginative illustrations to inform various industries about how Xerox could serve them. On the facing page is an example of the illustrations, this one geared to utilities.

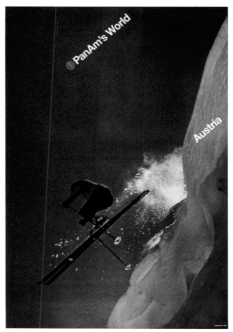

Another case of a global brand that we truncated to reflect everyday speech was **Pan American World Airways**, a leading American airline and a pioneer in international travel. Ticket offices had the full corporate name on the façade, but almost everyone referred to the company simply as **Pan Am**. We convinced them to shorten the name for advertising and promotion purposes and designed a very simple wordmark for Pan Am. This was joined with a world globe symbol to form a clear, concise identity.

Hundreds of items were designed using the updated identity. Among them was a large series of travel posters that featured commissioned photography by great photographers and a very minimal type treatment. The complete series, a few of which are shown here, are today in the permanent collection of The Museum of Modern Art.

Pan Am

The Smithsonian Institution had a major identity problem when it came to us in 1999: it was the world's largest national museum complex, with 19 museums, nine research institutes, and a vast diversity of exhibitions, catalogs, and products. And each of its museums used a different mark to identify itself. In addition, there was often no identification of the parent Smithsonian brand in their various communications.

Because the Smithsonian has increasingly had to augment its Congressional budget allocation with outside fundraising, it became essential to identify clearly and consistently each of the museums with the parent organization.

So when Secretary of the Smithsonian I. Michael Heyman asked Chermayeff & Geismar for help, it became clear to us that, in this case, our task would go well beyond traditional graphic design. Instead, we were to take part in reining in the leaderships of these various museums, who were used to projecting their own individual images.

We started with a comprehensive review of all the museums' communications, signs, magazines, posters, advertisements, labels, and packaging. What we found was utterly inconsistent identification. Some of the museums used versions of a sun symbol, but the length, number, and angle of the rays varied; the color of the sun was sometimes yellow, sometimes gold, or even red; and the blue background for the sky was never the same. Sometimes the sun was in a circle, sometimes not. There were 13 versions used frequently as well as many others used occasionally. Some didn't use a sun at all and instead used an unrelated mark. It was a mess.

The graphic design aspect of the solution was comparatively straightforward. When it came to selecting a single image to bring together all of the parts, we were convinced that the sun was the right choice. As mentioned, many of the subsidiaries used some form of the sun; the Smithsonian Institution itself traditionally had a sun for its mark, and so the sun image had considerable recognition and equity. Most important, however, the sun as a metaphor for knowledge just seemed appropriate for this national cultural and scientific organization.

Smithsonian
Anacostia Museum

Smithsonian
Archives of American Art

Smithsonian
Arthur M. Sackler Gallery

Smithsonian
Cooper-Hewitt, National Design Museum

Smithsonian
Freer Gallery of Art

Smithsonian
Hirshhorn Museum and Sculpture Garden

Smithsonian
National Air and Space Museum

Smithsonian
National Museum of African Art

Smithsonian
National Museum of American Art

Smithsonian
National Museum of American History

Smithsonian
National Museum of the American Indian

Smithsonian
National Museum of Natural History

Smithsonian
National Portrait Gallery

Smithsonian
National Postal Museum

Smithsonian
National Zoological Park

We redrew the sun, fixing the length and number of the rays, specifying one yellow and one blue. We locked up the new icon with the word "Smithsonian" written in Minion font and placed it on its own line, to be followed by the full formal name of the individual museum, set in italics.

Often traditional, pencil-to-paper graphic design has little to do with the task we are expected to perform. Once we solved the visual aspect of this problem, our scope was expanded beyond graphic design and into a general campaign to unite the Smithsonian bureaucracy. A collection of independent and powerful institutions naturally comes along with turf wars. Each museum director is generally an important and well-known personality in his or her own right, accustomed to being in charge of a large staff and controlling significant resources.

To avoid squabbling, Mike Heyman conspired with us to reach a consensus by arranging for each individual museum director to meet with us privately, two on one, never as a group.

The meetings took months to schedule. However, by meeting the museum directors individually, we treated them as feudal lords over their domains. On the other hand, any meeting with both the general director and an outside consultant brought a good deal of diplomatic pressure to bear on each head. In the end, we were able to convince everyone to come on board.

Ultimately, the Smithsonian's new mark was the means by which the institution's head clarified the relationship between the various museums and their parent institution in their public communications. Without the public really noticing the major identity changes that had to be adopted to put this iconic trademark system into place, the symbol, the wordmark, and the strict identity system have flourished successfully for many years.

The Smithsonian sun is now the public symbol of the institution's newfound unity—the end result of a rather complicated, if not to say chaotic, behind-the-scenes process.

(Previous page) Using the sun symbol and a distinctive typographic style, we created a consistent format for identifying the Smithsonian's various museums, galleries, and parks.

The Smithsonian identity is highly visible in the Washington, D.C. landscape. Goods sold at all Smithonian museum stores are carried out in shopping bags featuring the sun logo, and kiosk signs up and down the Mall feature the Smithsonian identity as well as those of the individual museums.

Smithsonian
Arthur M. Sackler
Gallery

through
April 13

EDO MASTERS FROM THE PRICE COLLECTION

Patterned Feathers
PIERCING EYES

For **Mobil**, the evolution to a spare, modern look emerged from a distinct change in personality and the recognition of a significant business opportunity.

While the name Mobiloil had long been a valuable and highly recognized trade name for the company's lubricants and fuels, the corporation's identity was less well defined. Until 1955 the company was known as the Socony Vacuum Oil Company ("Socony" being an acronym for Standard Oil Company of New York). In various other countries the name Vacuum Oil Company was used. The service station sign featured their famous flying red horse symbol in a shield.

In 1955, in its initial attempt to develop a more unified brand, the company adopted the name Socony Mobil and introduced a distorted shield-shaped identification sign featuring the word Mobil in very bold, dark lettering, hovering above a tiny red Pegasus. New service stations were painted a bright sky blue, and garish signs and banners filled the forecourt.

This was also a time when Americans were immigrating to the suburbs in increasing numbers. Oil companies such as Mobil found that they were being zoned out of new communities because of the less than graceful look of their service stations.

In recognition of this problem (and opportunity) and the desire to establish a single, unified global brand, the company decided in the mid-1960s to change its name worldwide to Mobil Oil Corporation and to develop a wide-ranging program to emphasize the Mobil trade name. At that time, Mobil felt that it had become a different kind of company, certainly a different kind of oil company and wanted the public to know who they were and what they stood for.

Architect Eliot Noyes was retained to design a modern service station concept and Chermayeff & Geismar to develop a new graphic identity for the company. Together the two firms undertook a comprehensive design program, initially focusing on developing a radically cleaner, more modern and attractive service station and related signs and packaging that would help Mobil become the service station of choice for newly developing communities. The concept worked, and Mobil leaped ahead of its competitors in winning choice locations from local zoning boards.

The idea of the red O came about partly to reinforce a design concept to use circular canopies, pumps, and display elements for a distinctive and attractive look. It also served to help people pronounce the name correctly (Mo-bil, not Mo-bile), and of course to add a single memorable and distinctive element to an otherwise very simple lettering style. At the same time, the flying red horse was removed from the sign, redrawn, and placed at a large size on the service station building itself. It didn't disappear; it was actually given more emphasis, but as a separate element.

Over the next 30-plus years, as the company's official graphics consultants, Chermayeff & Geismar developed a continually evolving and wide-ranging program of signs, packaging, print promotion, vehicle and equipment markings, safety signs, and color schemes for Mobil's worldwide operations. Throughout that time, and in spite of radical changes in the way products are packaged, sold, and dispensed, the graphics program remained consistent, based on four basic ideas that we first expressed in our initial presentation to Mobil management.

Previous trademark

Early sketch

Mobil

These four cornerstone elements are the Mobil trademark, in its distinctive colors and letterforms; the Pegasus symbol, on its white disk, as an important secondary trademark; the Mobil Alphabet, a distinctive, specially designed lettering style which acts as an extension of the Mobil trademark and is used in a single weight for all product names, signs, titles, and advertising headlines; and a distinctive family of colors, with a clear philosophy for how and when color is to be used. These four ideas were used in combination to create a consistent and recognizable appearance for all visual aspects of the company.

Signs, packaging, and equipment require considerable investment, and their designs need to be carefully developed and standardized, with clear guidelines established. On the other hand, for areas such as advertising and promotion, there were purposely never any fixed guidelines and grids, but rather only the requirement to use the Mobil Alphabet for all titles and headlines and to include the Mobil trademark as the signature. We took this approach recognizing that while advertising and promotion must reflect the same outlook as all other corporate expressions, it must also have a component of creativity and change of pace if it is to remain vital and effective. Without any rules there would be anarchy. But without creativity, there would be sterility and stagnation.

This approach was carried out over an unusually diverse communications program, from opinion messages in newspapers to extensive television advertising, from sporting events to sponsorship of numerous arts and cultural activities. It resulted in a wide array of powerful and groundbreaking work that, by implication, conveyed a sense of quality and progressiveness that was an essential goal of all Mobil's communications and furthered the company's desire to establish a clear picture of its unusual corporate personality.

The graphic treatment designed for all Mobil service stations featured a limited number of essential design components: the Mobil trademark; the flying red horse symbol on a white disk; the special Mobil type style used for all product names, promotional signs, and even the grade designations on the pumps; and a limited color palette that allowed only the most important features to stand out. This same approach was used for all product packaging. The Mobil 1 oil cans above are an example.

Imaginative use was made of the basic Mobil graphic identity elements, and especially the red *O* at the company's own facilities, where employees are the audience.

As shown on the facing page, a huge sliced red *O* sculpture marks the entrance to the corporation's headquarters in Fairfax, Virginia.

On this page, a twisting tower of red *Os* is in the landscape at the company's Princeton, New Jersey, research center.

And in a company office in Milton Keynes, England, a fractured logo tapestry is one of a series within an employees' stairwell.

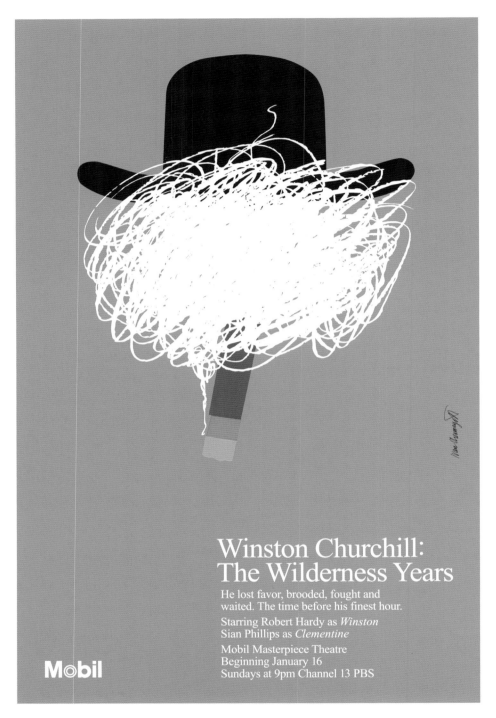

Winston Churchill:
The Wilderness Years

He lost favor, brooded, fought and
waited. The time before his finest hour.

Starring Robert Hardy as *Winston*
Sian Phillips as *Clementine*

Mobil Masterpiece Theatre
Beginning January 16
Sundays at 9pm Channel 13 PBS

Mobil

Over many years, as part of an extensive public-affairs effort, Mobil sponsored numerous cultural events and television shows. We created posters for a great many of these. The Churchill poster is one example of the hundreds shown in the book *Posters Made Possible by a Grant from Mobil*.

The cover we designed, shown on the facing page, features the corners of stacked posters from the book.

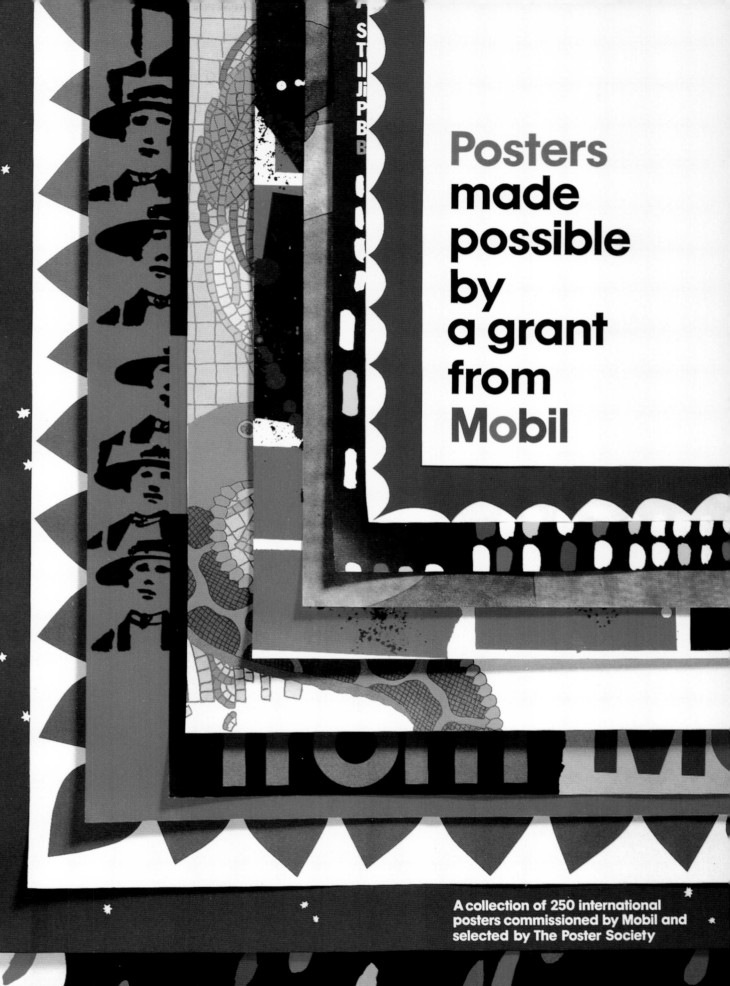

Posters made possible by a grant from Mobil

A collection of 250 international posters commissioned by Mobil and selected by The Poster Society

Index

Acknowledgments

We are immensely grateful for the preface written for this book by Isaac Mizrahi, which makes clear his insightful interest in visual communications and for the scholarly and moving foreward by Steven Heller.

We thank our editor Aaron Kenedi and our publisher F + W Media for taking *Identify* on as Print Publishing's first title and doing so without hesitation or limitations.

This project would not have been possible without Christopher Nutter of Nutter Media, who steered the book from its inception as literary agent, editorial advisor, and publicist.

Of course, we could not have completed this book without the assiduous assistance of our staff, Mirna Raduka, Anna Keeler, Arthur Beach, Melanie MacElduff, Gina Moreno Valle, Donna Driscoll, and Brendan Rooney, as well as Marilee Scott and Dave Barber, who helped greatly with the writing.

We would like to thank the hundreds of designers who have worked at the Chermayeff & Geismar office over the years, and most especially our former partner Steff Geissbuhler, for their considerable contribution to the work shown in this book.

We are forever grateful to our clients, past and present. Their support of design, sometimes over decades, has been extremely encouraging. We are especially grateful to the Koç family in Turkey; David Tieger, founder of Gemini Consulting; Jack Masey, former director of design for the USIA; Kerstin Scheuch, Director of Centro in Mexico City; Irene Chambers of the Library of Congress; Maro Chermayeff and Jeff Dupré of Show of Force; Hakuhodo in Tokyo; David Rockefeller; Sheldon Solow; Diana and Jonathan Rose; Ümit Taftali; Peter Chermayeff; Eliot Noyes, an early and loyal supporter; Richard Koshalek, director of the Hirshhorn Museum and Sculpture Garden; Jonathan Fanton, former President of the New School and the MacArthur Foundation; and Rawleigh Warner Jr., former chairman of Mobil Corporation, for their support. A special gratitude is extended to Gina Diez Barroso Franklin and Abraham Franklin.